"In a compelling series of letters Pastor Hedges do a fairly complex theological idea, perseverance of Often, it seemed many of the letters were actuall blessed, as I was, by reading this book."

— **BG Allen**, Team Leader for Ambassador Enterprises.

"This collection of letters packs a theological punch that will correct the false dichotomy that grace and effort are antithetical. Readers will be drawn in to engage thoughtfully the progression of the correspondence. And along the way, readers will be exposed to a wonderful array of instructive classic Christian literature—both fiction and nonfiction—that ought to be added to their 'books to read list,' if not to their own libraries."

— **Ardel B. Caneday**, Professor, University of Northwestern

"Every believer struggles to maintain the healthy balance between grace and good works. Brian Hedges, in a wonderful readable style, gives us the biblical insight and practical balance we need. This will be a book you read over and over again and give to those you're discipling. Some books don't help much; this one will lead you to a vibrant spiritual life!"

— **Bill Elliff**, Lead Pastor, The Summit Church in Little Rock, AK

"Biblically balanced, theologically precise, and warmly pastoral, *Active Spirituality* will counsel your mind, encourage your heart, and feed your soul. Chew on its nourishing truth and you are sure to grow as you pursue the holiness that can only be empowered by God's grace."

— **Paul Tautges**, Pastor, author, founder of Counseling One Another

"What Brian Hedges writes, I read. Why? Because his love for the beauty of God's grace is matched with his passion to see Christianity work in the real world. I need that! Once again Brian has served me and my church well by providing a fresh treatment of how our spiritual lives should work. What's more he's given it to us in a format of a friend: a series of letters. This book is a treasure of godly counsel for the daily journey of Christlikeness."

— **Mark Vroegop**, Lead Pastor, College Park Church, Indianapolis, Indiana

Active Spirituality

grace and effort in the christian life

BRIAN G. HEDGES

Shepherd Press
Wapwallopen, Pennsylvania

© 2014 *Active Spirituality* by Brian G. Hedges
Trade Paperback: ISBN 978-1-936908-57-8

ePub format ISBN: 978-1-936908-58-5
Mobi format ISBN: 978-1-936908-59-2

Published by Shepherd Press
P.O. Box 24
Wapwallopen, Pennsylvania 18660

All rights reserved. No part of this book may be reproduced or utilized in any form or by any means, electronic or mechanical, or by any information storage and retrieval system—except for brief quotations for the purpose of review, without written permission from the publisher.

Unless otherwise indicated, all Scripture are taken from The Holy Bible, English Standard Version. Copyright ©2001 by Crossway Bibles, a division of Good News Publishers. Used by permission. All rights reserved. Italics or bold text within Scripture quotations indicate emphasis added by author.

Page design and typesetting by Lakeside Design Plus
Cover design by Tobias' Outerwear for Books

First Printing, 2014
Printed in the United States of America

BP   26 25 24 23 22 21 20 19 18 17 16 15 14
15 14 13 12 11 10 9   8   7   6   5   4   3   2   1

Library of Congress Cataloging-in-Publication Data
Hedges, Brian G.
    Active spirituality : grace and effort in the Christian life / by Brian Hedges.
            pages cm
    ISBN 978-1-936908-57-8 (print book : alk. paper)—ISBN 978-1-936908-59-2 (mobi e-book)—ISBN 978-1-936908-58-5 (epub e-book) 1. Christian life. 2. Grace (Theology) 3. Reformed Church--Doctrines. I. Title.
    BV4501.3.H4335 2014
    248.4—dc23
                        2014008849

eBook Information: Go to: http://www.shepherdpress.com/ebooks

This book is lovingly dedicated to my grandparents,
Arthur and Mozelle Hedges

Contents

Opening Letter

Dear Reader,

This is a book about two things that at first glance may seem incompatible: grace and effort. We don't usually put those two words together. When we think of grace, we tend to emphasize what God has done over what we must do.

Grace *versus* works, right?

It is good and right to emphasize God's work of grace *for* us when we're thinking about how to get right with God. Justification is by grace alone, through faith alone, in Christ alone. Nothing you have done, nor anything you can do, can contribute anything to the saving righteousness of Jesus.

> Not the labors of my hands
> Can fulfill thy law's demands;
> Could my zeal no respite know,
> Could my tears forever flow,
> All for sin could not atone;
> Thou must save, and Thou alone.

The recent resurgence of Reformed theology has allowed many to rediscover this dimension of grace, and that is a great gain. People who grew up thinking that Christianity mainly consists of dos and don'ts hear this reemphasis on the gospel of free grace as truly good news. There is nothing quite so liberating as coming to rest in the finished work of Christ!

Along with this rediscovery has come a flashflood of books about the "gospel" and how it changes and transforms us. I certainly haven't read all of these books (though I did write one of them!), but from what I can tell, the underlying emphasis seems to be something like this: these writers want you to understand that you're not only justified by faith alone, but you're also sanctified by faith alone. They want to celebrate how the gospel is the only way a lost person becomes saved, but also how it's the only way a saved person grows and matures. These books remind us that transformation, no less than justification, is driven by the gospel, empowered by grace, and centered on Christ alone.

Amen. I agree. Keep preaching, my New Calvinist comrades!

Dangers to the North and the South

But (you knew a "but" was coming, didn't you?) I do think a caution is in order because this emphasis on grace *can* sound like a dismissal of effort. These books *can* sound like they're pitting grace *against* works. The church does not easily live in the middle ground where both grace *and* effort dwell.

To explain, let me borrow and adapt an image from C. S. Lewis's magnificent allegory *The Pilgrim's Regress*. If you think of the Christian life as a journey across a rugged terrain, there are significant dangers to both the north and the south.

To the frozen north are the arctic dangers of icy legalism and frigid formalism, where religiosity and self-righteousness freeze the heart, leaving us brittle, cold, and hard towards both God and fellow human beings. The church veers north when she loses her wonder at the *freedom* of grace, when the heart-warming doctrine of justification by faith alone slips from her grasp.

But to the swampy south, there are the tropical dangers of sultry self-indulgence and lazy licentiousness, where grace is twisted into license, and even biblically-warranted, faith-fueled effort is condemned as legalism. Bonhoeffer called this "cheap grace." (The theological word for it is *antinomianism*, which means *against law*.) The church wanders south when she loses her wonder at the *power* of grace; neglects the biblical demands for effort, perseverance, and watchfulness; and collapses the action-laden language of the New Testament (walk, fight, run, conquer, etc.) into overly simple, reductionist formulas that vacate sanctifying faith of all effort.

While the doctrine of justification by faith alone rescues us from the frozen glacier of legalism, it's the doctrine of the perseverance of the saints that liberates us from the miry bog of antinomianism.

At its heart, this book is about the perseverance of the saints.

The Perseverance of the Saints Defined

A definition may be in order at this point. After all, the phrase "perseverance of the saints" is a theological mouthful that ordinary Christians don't often use. So, when I speak of the perseverance of the saints, what do I mean?

In good preacherly fashion, let me first offer a single sentence definition, followed by three clarifications, and then (since pictures are worth a thousand words) an illustration.

The definition: *The perseverance of the saints means that true believers cannot lose their salvation but will persevere in faith to the end and be saved.*

Now, the clarifications: (1) This does not mean that a believer can live in perpetual sin, without repentance, and still be saved. Some people equate the doctrine of perseverance with a somewhat stripped-down version of it usually dubbed "eternal security" or "the security of the believer" (the doctrine that a believer cannot lose his or her salvation). And some proponents of eternal security go so far as to say that a true, born-again Christian can even quit believing altogether but still remain eternally saved.

But the classic Reformed understanding of perseverance, while certainly affirming the eternal security of a genuine believer, says more. The doctrine of perseverance also clarifies what kind of faith is saving faith, since it recognizes that Scripture itself contrasts true faith against a kind of faith that is false (see James 2). Therefore, the doctrine of perseverance teaches *both* that a true believer cannot lose his or her salvation *and* that a true believer will persevere in faith and holiness.

(2) That said, true believers can and often do still sin. Let's be honest. I do, and so do you. Sometimes believers even fall into serious sin. The Reformed confessions are clear on this point. For example, one old confession (The London Baptist Confession, 1689) says that Christians "may, through the temptation of Satan and of the world, the prevalency of corruption remaining in them, and the neglect of means of their preservation, fall into grievous sins, and for a time continue therein."

This can lead to severe consequences in a believer's life. That same confession goes on to say that through such failure, believers "incur God's displeasure, and grieve his Holy Spirit, come to have their graces and comforts impaired, have their hearts hardened, and their consciences wounded, hurt and scandalize others, and bring temporal judgments upon themselves."

In other words, the doctrine of perseverance is painfully realistic about both the sins and failures of Christians and the terrible consequences this can unleash in a person's life. Even in acknowledging these dangers, however, there is the underlying assurance that true believers "yet shall . . . renew their repentance and be preserved through faith in Christ Jesus to the end."

(3) Finally, while we need to emphasize the responsibility of believers to believe, obey, endure, persevere, and be holy, we must never forget that all of this ultimately depends on God's grace. Yes, we are commanded to "keep [ourselves] in the love of God" (Jude v. 21), but we can only keep ourselves because of "him who is able to keep [us] from stumbling and to present [us] blameless before the presence of his glory with great joy" (Jude v. 24).

Maybe an illustration will help. The life of a Christian has sometimes been compared to the Mississippi River. The general flow of The Big Muddy is from north to south, but anyone who looks at a map will see that sometimes the river flows east or west, and in at least one place even turns north for a short while. Despite these many sideways and occasional backwards turns, the water always eventually flows south.

In a similar way, while believers generally increase in faith and holiness, they certainly take many detours to the right or left, sometimes even temporarily turning away from the Lord into deeper patterns of sin and disobedience. But the firmness of God's love, the strength of his grace, the effectiveness of Christ's death, the power of his prayers, and the sway of his Spirit in our hearts guarantees that our God will always and eventually draw us back to himself in repentant faith.

The Need for an Active Spirituality

This book, like my previous two, is born from my own struggles to understand and practice the Christian life. The dangers to north and south are not just dangers for the church at large but for each individual believer. More often than I care to admit, I have found myself subtly slipping first one way, then the other—towards self-righteousness and rigidity on the one hand or self-indulgence and passivity on the other.

Studying the various New Testament metaphors for living the Christian life has helped me in this struggle. I find the strongly action-oriented nature of these images almost startling: the Christian life is called a walk, a race, a contest, and a fight. We are told to run, to wrestle, to watch, and to stand. And the victors—those who conquer and overcome—receive great promises whereas terrible warnings go to those who grow sluggish and neglect the great salvation secured for us by Jesus.

Some of these metaphors formed the original idea for this book, but over time, some other pieces came into play. I started thinking about the nature of backsliding and apostasy and the specific sin of sloth or acedia (one of the classic seven deadly sins). Then there was the perennial question of how to live in the world without either idolizing it or becoming a pleasure-denying ascetic.

These issues, even more than the problems in faulty theological systems, caused me to see my own need for a very real, robust spirituality.

In other words, I've not written this book simply because Christians need balanced theology (as important as that is) but because there are real threats and dangers to my life and faith, and to yours. I want to be standing in Christ ten years from now. And I won't be unless (by God's grace) my spirituality is active.

Oswald Chambers said it well: "If we are going to live as disciples of Jesus, we have to remember that all efforts of worth and excellence are difficult. The Christian life is gloriously difficult, but its difficulty does not make us faint and cave in—it rouses us up to overcome. Do we appreciate the miraculous salvation of Jesus Christ enough to be our utmost for His highest—our best for His glory?"

Letters of Spiritual Counsel

This book may seem unusual in its form. Rather than writing a linear, deductive, step-by-step primer on the active metaphors of the New Testament (what I'd originally planned), I've written a series of letters. There are a couple of reasons for this.

First, I thought it would be a fun and creative approach to writing theology. With the advent of the Internet, email, and texting, it appears that the art of letter writing has passed. But I'm old enough to remember both the quiet reflection involved in writing letters and the unique thrill of receiving them. While I like the new technologies, I view the decline of letter writing as a significant loss. Church history is rich with letters that were uniquely pastoral in character. Think of Martin Luther's *Letters of Spiritual Counsel,* John Newton's *Cardiphonia,* or C. S. Lewis's more widely read *The Screwtape Letters* and *Letters to Malcolm: Chiefly on Prayer.* And the richest spiritual letters we have are in the New Testament: Spirit-breathed letters by the apostles.

I certainly do not disdain newer forms of technology (I often use them!), but I think letter writing can still serve both individuals and the church. Hence, the form of this book.

There's a second reason I wrote this book as a series of letters. Our faith journeys are not linear or direct from infancy to maturity, from ignorance to understanding, from earth to heaven (or better, to the New Heavens and New Earth). No, our journeys are circuitous and roundabout, with lots of detours and obstacles, punctuated by backtracking, rest stops, and significant delays on the side of the road.

So these letters don't begin with the concept of "active spirituality" and then move sequentially through the need for it, the reasons for it, the character of it, etc. How unrealistic (and boring) a book like that would be! No, these are letters written to someone in the throes of temptation and endurance, agony and ecstasy, victory and defeat. They are written to a struggling young adult trying to find a church, live a chaste life, and walk with Jesus. In other words, these letters are not just theological—they are pastoral, written to help believers apply Christian theology to the complexities of real life.

You will hear echoes of other Christian writers in this book. They are my conversation partners as I try to work out a practical life of faith. They include John Bunyan, whose *Pilgrim's Progress* has instructed and encouraged me since my childhood. Then there's C. S. Lewis, whose writings have baptized my imagination; I learned from him (and Saint Augustine) the importance of rightly-ordered loves that can embrace all created goods under the lordship of Christ. John Owen's rich books of pastoral theology feed, instruct, rebuke, and encourage me like no others, so I am apt to quote them often when trying to encourage others. And, finally, Thomas Schreiner and Ardel Caneday first opened up to me the biblical metaphor of "the race" and its relationship to persevering faith in their excellent book *The Race Set Before Us: A Biblical Theology of Perseverance and Assurance*. Few books have had a more profound shaping influence on my understanding of the Christian life, so it plays a big part in how I have crafted these letters.

A few explanatory comments are probably in order. First, while I have written these letters to "Chris" (Christian) as realistically as possible, they are fictional. I've written them in my own voice, and all of the significant autobiographical details are true of me, but I do claim creative license for some incidental details, which I've sometimes invented or changed for the sake of interest. The letters do build on one another and follow an implicit storyline, so you should read them in order rather than skip around. And to provide a smoother reading experience, I've chosen not to include footnotes to quotations and references in the letters themselves; if you want that information, see the Notes section at the end of the book.

Exploring the Depths

One athletic image that Paul did not use in his letters, but serves well as a metaphor for this book, is scuba diving. Perhaps Paul would have used it, had it been invented. For just as *walking* captures the persevering, and sometimes plodding, nature of our pilgrimage in the journey of faith; and *fighting* vividly portrays the violent realities of our conflicted warfare with sin and Satan; and *running* pictures our endurance as we press forward to grasp the heavenly prize; so *diving* depicts our attempts to probe the depth and mystery of God's grace. And, in fact, Paul does exult in "the *depth* of the riches and wisdom and knowledge of God" (Romans 11:33) and reminds us that the "Spirit searches everything, even the *depths* of God" (1 Corinthians 2:10). One of my hopes as you dive into these pages is that the Spirit will grant you a deeper understanding of the mystery of how God's grace works in our disciplined effort and through our personal experiences to more closely conform us into the image of Christ.

None of us fully understand the journey we're signing up for when we first begin to follow Christ. We all encounter obstacles for which we are unprepared. Among our fellow travelers are companions who strengthen our faith and help us along the way, while others can get us off track. We face hostile enemies, including the toxic idolatries of this present evil age, the subtle and deceptive temptations of dark spiritual powers, and the fierce outposts of remaining sin in our own hearts. All of these conspire to sabotage our faith. But the gospel promises that God's grace is far greater than the combined force of all our foes. By faith, we can rest in knowing that every ounce of holy effort we exert is itself the fruit of God's grace. Whatever effort we make flows from the sovereign, unbreakable love of our Father; the effectual, finished work of our prophet, priest, and king, Jesus, the Son of God; and the mighty and mysterious power of the indwelling Spirit. In the words of an old hymn,

> Every virtue we possess,
> And every conquest won,
> And every thought of holiness,
> Are His alone.

Walking in the Way

Dear Chris,

It was really great to get your letter yesterday. I'm glad we had a chance to talk over coffee a few weeks ago. You have some important decisions ahead of you, and I'll be praying for the Lord's guidance, especially as it relates to your career and finding a new church family. Remember that his guidance extends beyond these big life-altering decisions into the nitty-gritty details of your daily attitudes, routines, and habits. To use the biblical words, the Lord is concerned with how we *walk* and with all of our *ways*.

Last summer, my three oldest kids (you may remember that we have four) and I discovered a great hiking trail just a few miles from where we live. It's a trail through the woods that winds in and out of several parks just on the east side of the St. Joseph River, complete with a river shelter and several picnic areas and playgrounds just off the trail. The kids were enthralled, and our little hike led into a natural conversation about walking the right path or *way* in life.

The word *walk* is one of the main biblical metaphors for living the Christian life. Sometimes I think its significance is lost on us today. In the ancient world, walking was the ordinary person's primary mode of transportation. The best way to get from here to there was to walk. They didn't have trains, planes, and automobiles—even the bicycle wasn't invented until the nineteenth century! Horses, at least in ancient Israel, were scarce and primarily used in battle. So most journeys were taken on foot by walking. We see this especially in the life of Jesus. As someone once noted, Jesus is the most persistent pedestrian in the Bible!

So the idea of *walking* in a *way* was the perfect picture for an ancient person to understand the moral and spiritual life. We find the metaphor early in Genesis where God walked in the garden of

Eden in the cool of the day (Genesis 3:8), picturing God's active presence with humanity in their original created state. That fellowship was interrupted, of course, by the fall. But as the redemption story unfolds, God once again walks with his people. "I will walk among you and be your God," God says to Israel (Leviticus 26:12).

He not only walks with us, but we walk with him. Both Enoch and Noah are commended for walking with God (Genesis 5:22, 24; 6:9), and the Lord said to Abraham, "I am God Almighty; walk before me, and be blameless" (Genesis 17:1). The New Testament has many instances of this imagery as well. John and Paul describe Christian behavior in terms of walking in light rather than darkness, walking as Jesus walked, walking in wisdom, walking in newness of life, walking in good works, walking in the Spirit, and so on.

But to walk, one must have a way, a road, or a path. The Scriptures are full of this imagery, and it is especially obvious in Old Testament poetry, wisdom literature, and the prophetic books. The first psalm contrasts the ways of the righteous and wicked, commending the man who "walks not in the counsel of the wicked, nor stands in the way of sinners, nor sits in the seat of scoffers" (Psalm 1:1). The first verse of Psalm 119 echoes that commendation, declaring the blessedness of "those whose way is blameless, who walk in the law of the Lord," while Proverbs 4:18 says that "the path of the righteous is like the light of dawn, which shines brighter and brighter until full day." Later, Jesus taught about discipleship and salvation by contrasting the hard way that leads to life with the easy way that leads to destruction (Matthew 7:13–14), and Luke describes the early Christians as followers of "the Way" (Acts 9:2; 19:9, 23; 22:4; 24:14, 22).

This brief survey of *walk* and *way* imagery in Scripture (and there are dozens and dozens of other texts—I encourage you to search them out.) suggests several insights about Christian living:

(1) First of all, it involves effort, movement, and action. Walking requires motion, and so does following Jesus. The Christian life is not a passive or static state. Ours is an active spirituality.

(2) But it also involves choices. You must choose a road, a path, a way in which to walk. The Scriptures variously describe this path as

a way of life, light, love, truth, righteousness, etc. But what is clear is that there is a *way* that leads to salvation and a *way* that doesn't.

The Pilgrim's Progress, John Bunyan's classic allegory about the journey of faith, vividly captures this reality. I love this book and think it is worth repeated readings. Spurgeon reportedly read it over a hundred times! I haven't read it a hundred times, but I do keep coming back to it. I recently realized that Bunyan not only describes the Christian's journey through life with all its attending obstacles, detours, and dangers, but also provides a startling array of characters to illustrate defective faith. It's a study in apostasy every bit as much as it is a portrayal of the perseverance of the saints. When we meet Obstinate, Pliable, Ignorance, Hypocrisy, Worldly Wiseman, Talkative, Formalist, Legality, and all the rest, we're not just encountering transparent examples of unbelievers and apostates. We're also seeing in detail the kinds of spiritual problems that get people off track. The one thing all of these characters have in common is that they didn't continue walking in the way to the Celestial City.

(3) Therefore, we must keep walking in the right way. Whenever we realize we've gotten off the path, we must by God's grace find the way back on. Bunyan's Christian does this again and again, and he makes it all the way home only with dogged persistence. So must you and I. The most fatal thing is to stop walking.

(4) Finally, both Scripture and Bunyan remind us that walking often involves companionship. We must walk with the Lord (Genesis 5:22; Revelation 3:4), but we must also walk with others who follow him: "Whoever walks with the wise becomes wise, but the companion of fools will suffer harm" (Proverbs 13:20). Christian met numerous cases of dubious character and doubtful faith, but he also had companions like Faithful and Hopeful who helped him in the journey.

Like Christian, we also need good spiritual companions. Don't underestimate the importance of true Christian fellowship for your life. It will make a huge difference in your spiritual progress.

Your fellow pilgrim,
Brian

Turning to God

Dear Chris,

I forgot to actually answer your question and say yes, I'd love to keep in touch more consistently . . . but I hope that was obvious from my last letter. Writing has always been a help to my spiritual life as well, and I've really enjoyed our friendship over the years.

Sometimes we pastors and theologians forget to define our terms! Thanks for asking for the clarification. By *perseverance of the saints*, I mean the classic Reformation doctrine that teaches both the security of the believer and the necessity of persistent, ongoing faith. Bunyan's story is the best primer on perseverance, precisely because it is a story. You should definitely read it! Given the ideas you want to discuss, I'm sure I'll be referring to it again and again.

As I've been thinking about your initial letter and the many questions you asked, I keep returning to the many metaphors that Scripture gives us for living the Christian life: *walk* (as I discussed in my last letter), *turn, fight, run, grow, conquer,* and more. The biblical writers were concrete thinkers, and they've given us vivid images to help us understand the spiritual life.

One of the most important of these active verbs is *turn*. The Christian life begins with turning. See Paul's description of believers in 1 Thessalonians 1:9: "You turned to God from idols to serve the living and true God." This is one of the classic biblical descriptions of conversion. And notice how it involves both turning *from* and turning *to*: "you turned from idols to . . . God." See also Acts 26:18, which speaks of turning from darkness to light and from Satan to God.

This teaches us that Christian conversion is a necessary change of one's entire orientation and outlook. While once we were oriented towards the darkness of idolatry and sin, now we gaze on the marvelous light of God's glory revealed in the face of Christ his Son.

Conversion involves a change of masters. Once we served idols, and through them, Satan; now we serve God in Christ.

But turning to God isn't a onetime affair. Conversion is not a point but a line. We never outgrow our need for repentance. We must turn from sin to Christ over and over again. That's why Luther was right in saying, "When our Lord and Master, Jesus Christ, said 'Repent', He called for the entire life of believers to be one of penitence."

I say all of this for three reasons. First, to encourage you that your present battles with sin do not mean that you are not a Christian. I wouldn't presume to give you assurance, as only the Holy Spirit can do that. But I do want to steer you away from thinking that the presence of sin or the experience of conflict indicates a lack of salvation.

I also suspect that you have some "heart work" to do, to borrow a phrase from the past. You wrote of "a strangeness" between you and God—a painful feeling that I know only too well. We can feel this estrangement from God for various reasons, not just because of sin. And woe to the counselor who assumes that all afflictions are chastisements for sin! Remember Job's miserable comforters. Nevertheless, as you seek to "rekindle the dying embers of [your] faith," you will need to practice the disciplines of self-examination and repentance.

But, finally, let me stress the "turning to" aspect of conversion. You may need to take "inventory" of your sins, as you say, but you certainly shouldn't linger there for too long. There is a dangerous kind of pietism that overkills on soul-searching and introspection, to the neglect of outgoing faith in Jesus. As the old theologian Thomas Watson once said, "Spiritual sorrow will sink the heart if the pulley of faith does not raise it." Beware of analysis paralysis!

Remember, you are turning *to* Jesus—the Friend of Sinners, the Lover of your soul. Let that be your focus.

I'm eager to hear from you again soon. Feel free to call me as well—you have my number.

Brian

P.S. Have you read Tim Keller's article "All of Life is Repentance"? It's one of the most succinct and helpful guides for personal self-examination and repentance I've seen. As with so much of what he writes, Keller draws a careful distinction between genuine gospel repentance and the common counterfeit—a kind of religious repentance that is "self-righteous" and "bitter all the way down." Then he uses a quotation from George Whitefield as a matrix for gospel-oriented self-examination. I've pasted this portion of the article below:

> In a January 9, 1738, letter to a friend, George Whitefield laid out an order for regular repentance. (He ordinarily did his inventory at night.) He wrote: "God give me a deep humility and a burning love, a well-guided zeal and a single eye, and then let men and devils do their worst!" Here is one way to use this order in gospel-grounded repentance.

Deep humility (vs. pride)

> Have I looked down on anyone? Have I been too stung by criticism? Have I felt snubbed and ignored?
>
> Repent like this: Consider the free grace of Jesus until I sense a) decreasing disdain (since I am a sinner too), b) decreasing pain over criticism (since I should not value human approval over God's love.) In light of his grace I can let go of the need to keep up a good image—it is too great a burden and now unnecessary. Consider free grace until I experience grateful, restful joy.

Burning love (vs. indifference)

> Have I spoken or thought unkindly of anyone? Am I justifying myself by caricaturing (in my mind) someone else? Have I been impatient and irritable? Have I been self-absorbed and indifferent and inattentive to people?
>
> Repent like this: Consider the free grace of Jesus until there is a) no coldness or unkindness (think of the sacrificial love of Christ for you), b) no impatience (think of his patience with you), and c) no indifference. Consider free grace until I show warmth and affection. God was infinitely patient and attentive to me, out of grace.

Wise courage (vs. anxiety)

Have I avoided people or tasks that I know I should face? Have I been anxious and worried? Have I failed to be circumspect or have I been rash and impulsive?

Repent like this: Consider the free grace of Jesus until there is a) no cowardly avoidance of hard things (since Jesus faced evil for me), b) no anxious or rash behavior (since Jesus' death proves God cares and will watch over me). It takes pride to be anxious—I am not wise enough to know how my life should go. Consider free grace until I experience calm thoughtfulness and strategic boldness.

Godly motivations (a "single eye")

Am I doing what I am doing for God's glory and the good of others or am I being driven by fears, need for approval, love of comfort and ease, need for control, hunger for acclaim and power, or the "fear of man"? Am I looking at anyone with envy? Am I giving in to any of even the first motions of lust or gluttony? Am I spending my time on urgent things rather than important things because of these inordinate desires?

Repent like this: How does Jesus provide for me what I am looking for in these other things? Pray: "O Lord Jesus, make me happy enough in you to avoid sin and wise enough in you to avoid danger, that I may always do what is right in your sight, in your name I pray, Amen."

The Noonday Demon

Dear Chris,

As always, I was glad to get your letter yesterday. I really appreciate how honest you are with your struggles and doubts. And I'll do my best to offer help, though the best thing I can do is pray.

I think you've encountered what one of the desert fathers called "the noonday demon"—that insidious, listless state of mind that masquerades as weariness (that's why it's listed among the seven deadly sins as "sloth") but at its root is apathy towards God and spiritual things.

The Greek name for it is *acedia*, which means "without care." (I doubt you're presently much concerned with Greek terms—or church history for that matter! But as with all maladies of the soul, we can learn much from our spiritual ancestors. Their capacity for reflection and self-knowledge often exceeds our own, even though we are citizens of the Age of the Self.)

R. R. Reno wrote a great article in *First Things* that described acedia as "a lassitude and despair that overwhelms spiritual striving," and he surveyed spiritual writing about this sin throughout Christian history. Bernard of Clairvaux speaks of a *sterilitas animae*, a sterility, dryness, and barrenness of his soul that makes the sweet honey of psalm-singing seem tasteless and turns vigils into empty trials. Medieval English writers often speak of acedia as wanhope, a waning of confidence in the efficacy and importance of prayer. For Dante, on the fourth ledge of purgatory, those afflicted by acedia are described as suffering from *lento amore*, a slow love that cannot motivate and uplift, leaving the soul stagnant, unable to move under the heavy burden of sin.

Of course, you know that I'm not a huge fan of monasticism, nor do I believe in purgatory. But I find this kaleidoscope of descriptions of acedia quite helpful. Dryness and sterility of soul. Waning hope. Slow love. Inability to move. According to Reno, this "noonday devil tempts us into a state of spiritual despair and sadness that drains us of our Christian hope." This sounds like the condition you described to me in your letter. And it's a spiritual disorder that I have also found in myself. Not all the time, but often enough to empathize and, hopefully, to help.

In my experience, the temptation to spiritual sloth seems strongest when overcommitment and busyness coincide with my slacking off in spiritual disciplines. The physical weariness seems to seep into my soul and leave me with a kind of lethargy or languor of the heart that at the moment feels almost impossible to shake. I can barely read or pray, much less meditate. Serving others becomes intolerably draining. And though I wish I could simply snap my fingers and make this torpor evaporate and go away, I feel enveloped in a thick fog of indifference. It does usually lift. Sometimes through reading the Psalms or in apparent answer to a barely murmured prayer. Sometimes after a change of scenery or getting some rest.

Not all Christians face this. And those who do may not experience it in the same way. I sometimes wonder if acedia now manifests itself more in frittering time away on smartphones and the Internet, in channel surfing and incessant talkativeness, than in the agonies of soul that Dante and Bernard and Spurgeon wrote about. Dorothy Sayers, in a piercing essay called "The Other Six Deadly Sins," said "one of the favorite tricks of this sin is to dissemble itself under cover of a whiffling activity of body." In other words, spiritual sloth is often camouflaged as restlessness and busyness.

But for many of us, myself included, acedia is a temptation stealthily targeted to an introverted, melancholy disposition. The isolated temptations are awful, but bearable. What's worse is when the stupor settles and hardens into an ongoing condition.

Incidentally, the very fact that you wrote to me about it is hopeful. I can imagine that it took enormous effort to put pen to paper and describe your heart so fully and so honestly. That alone is a mercy from the Lord. My first encouragement to you, then, is to remind you that our Father has not forsaken you! "He who began a good work in you will bring it to completion at the day of Jesus Christ" (Philippians 1:6). The old Calvinist doctrine of the perseverance of the saints is true, and I'll surely have more to say about it in later letters. But undergirding that faithful teaching is the doctrine of *God's* perseverance with the saints! He is persevering with you, my friend. Yes, he calls us to exercise holy effort as we run the race set before us, but all our effort is fueled by his grace: "Work out your own salvation with fear and trembling, *for it is God who works in you, both to will and to work for his good pleasure*" (Philippians 2:12–13).

Bunyan provides the perfect picture of this in *The Pilgrim's Progress*. In the Interpreter's House, Christian sees a fireplace in which flames burned "higher and hotter" even though someone kept dousing the fire with water to quench it. Christian asks his guide what this means, and the Interpreter answers, "This Fire is the Work of Grace that is wrought in the heart; he that casts water up on it, to extinguish and put it out, is the *Devil*." Then he takes the pilgrim to the other side of the wall, where he sees "a Man with a Vessel of Oil in his hand, of which he did continually cast (but secretly) into the Fire." When Christian again asks what this means, the Interpreter answers, "This is *Christ*, who continually with the Oil of his Grace maintains the work already begun in the heart: By the means of which, notwithstanding what the Devil can do, the souls of his people prove gracious still."

Though I have more to share with you that I believe will help you, I leave you with Bunyan's image and God's unfailing mercy. I will write again soon.

Prayerfully,
Brian

P.S. What are you reading these days? I always enjoy discussing books and find that shared reading is one of the great secrets to strong friendship.

Walking in the Spirit

Dear Chris,

Yes, I definitely share your enthusiasm for all things C. S. Lewis. I remember now that Lewis came up when we first met over coffee several years ago. No wonder we hit it off so quickly! I just read *Screwtape Letters* again for the fifth or sixth time and am glad to hear you're reading it too, though I think my favorite is *The Great Divorce*. Have you read it yet?

Following up on my letter from several weeks ago on the *walk* metaphor in Scripture, I wanted to say something about walking in the Spirit. It's interesting that while Paul uses the Old Testament imagery of walking, he distances himself from the law itself, in which the old covenant believers were commanded to walk: "Blessed are those whose way is blameless, who walk in the law of the Lord!" (Psalm 119:1).

Paul doesn't say this because he thinks that the law is bad, even though some people seemed to accuse him of that. In fact, he took great pains to argue that "the law is holy, and the commandment is holy and righteous and good" (Romans 7:12). But in that same context, he shows that the effect of the good and holy law on sinful human beings is not to restrain sin, much less cure it. Instead, the law arouses sin and leads to death (see Romans 7:7–11).

Paul realized that though the law portrays holiness for us, it can't make us holy. Though it shows us what sin looks like, it can't cleanse our hearts of sin. Instead, it just stirs up the corruption in our hearts.

So we need something more. We need the Spirit. That's why Paul says "we are released from the law, having died to that which held us captive, so that we serve in the *new way of the Spirit* and not in the old way of the written code" (Romans 7:6). This all comes about because of our union with Christ, of course. And I think this accounts for why Paul emphasizes walking *in the Spirit* (Galatians 5:16).

This means that as Christians we walk not in the old way of the Letter, but the new way of the Spirit. And the *power* in which we walk is not our own power, but the power of the Spirit. Look at 2 Corinthians 3 and Hebrews 8 for more contrasts between law and Spirit, old covenant and new.

I don't know how far you've gotten in *Pilgrim's Progress* yet, but there's a scene I always remember when I think about the function and limits of God's law. In the Interpreter's house, Christian sees "a very large parlour that was full of dust, because never swept." A man comes in and begins sweeping the room, but the stirred up dust almost chokes Christian. A young woman then sprinkles the room with water, "which when she had done was swept and cleansed with pleasure." When Christian asks Interpreter what it means, he learns that the parlour represents the human heart, while the dust is his "Original Sin, and inward Corruptions that have defiled the whole man." The man who tried to sweep the room represents the law, which "instead of cleansing the heart . . . from Sin" only stirs it up more. The woman, on the other hand, shows us the cleansing power of the gospel, which sprinkles the heart with grace, so that sin is "vanquished and subdued, and the soul made clean . . . and consequently fit for the King of Glory to inhabit."

Bunyan illustrates what Paul teaches in Romans 7: the law can show us our sin, but it cannot cleanse our hearts. More than this, we belong to the new covenant, not the old. We are not under the law, but under grace. This doesn't give us license to sin (see Romans 6), but it does mean we're in a different and better place in salvation history than Enoch, Noah, Abraham, and David. We've been given more!

An old poem puts it like this:

> Run, John, run, the law commands
> But gives us neither feet nor hands,
>
> Far better news the gospel brings:
> It bids us fly and gives us wings!

Walking with God, then, is not something we do in our own unaided, self-generated strength. The Christian life demands our effort and participation, but God's own Spirit energizes and fuels the effort it demands. The discipline God requires depends on the grace of his Spirit dwelling within us. We must serve, but "by the strength that God supplies" (1 Peter 4:11).

This means that one of the top priorities of the Christian life is learning to daily depend on the Spirit. What does that look like? It's kind of nebulous and hard to grasp, I know. Are we supposed to sit and wait for a feeling? Does the Spirit zap us with some kind of holy buzz? Do our own minds and wills at some point "switch off" when the Spirit "takes over"? That's certainly the impression that some versions of holiness teaching can give. I remember the lyrics of a song from several decades ago:

> It's not in trying, but in trusting
> It's not in running, but in resting
> Not in wondering, but in praying
> That we find the strength of the Lord.

Though that initially sounds good, somehow it doesn't quite fit the biblical picture. Doesn't Scripture not only invite us to rest, but also command us to run (Hebrews 12:1)?

No, the way of the Spirit doesn't eliminate the need for effort. On the contrary, the New Testament indicates that the work of the Spirit within us leads to *more* effort on our part—not less. Paul, you may recall, always exhorts the churches to more love, more knowledge, and more holiness.

Lewis, by the way, was also on the mark in *Letters to Malcolm:* "The deeper the level within ourselves from which our prayer, or any other act, wells up, the more it is His, but not at all the less ours. Rather, most ours when most His." That's the paradox! While grace is opposed to works in any kind of legalistic sense of earning favor with God, it isn't opposed to our action and effort. Grace rather produces our effort, and sustains it.

The Puritan John Owen, in his *magnum opus* on the Holy Spirit, said much the same: "The Holy Spirit so worketh *in us* as that he worketh *by us,* and what he doth in us is done by us. Our duty is to apply ourselves unto his commands, according to the conviction of our minds; and his work is to enable us to perform them."

But perhaps no one has said it better than Jonathan Edwards: "We are not merely passive in [efficacious grace], nor yet does God do some and we do the rest, but God does all and we do all. God produces all and we act all. For that is what he produces, our own acts. God is the only proper author and fountain; we only are the proper actors. We are in different respects wholly passive and wholly active."

So walk in the Spirit, my friend. In daily dependence on divine grace, actively choose to follow Jesus with all the passion and energy that *he* musters within you! Don't simply try to do better with an eye on the law. And don't sit idly by, waiting for some mystical jolt of power. Instead, prayerfully submit yourself to the Spirit and ask for his help. Then, get up, get going, and walk with God!

Brian

P.S. How is the search for a church going? I'm praying hard that you'll find the right church soon.

Counterfeit Faith

Dear Chris,

This afternoon I received your letter from last week. I suppose the holidays are responsible for slowing down the mail. I sent you a letter this morning, but it was obviously written before I received yours. In any case, I'll slow down my writing frenzy in order to give you time to respond, so that our letters won't always be crossing one another.

Yes, I agree actual letter writing has some distinct advantages over email. I've grown to dislike email more and more, to be honest. I suppose it's because I get so much. But it's also because it's so easy to send hasty emails and regret them later. This is a painful lesson for a pastor to learn. The less hurried nature of actual letter writing seems to encourage more careful thought. I also love writing with fountain pens, though I type so much faster than writing by hand.

As to your comment about apostasy, it hadn't occurred to me to suppose that Bunyan was describing true believers when writing about Talkative, Ignorance, and the others. And I really do think that you're wrong, both about Bunyan and in your interpretation of Scripture on this point. Have you read *Pilgrim's Progress* through to the end? It concludes with the Shining Ones depositing Ignorance in Hell! And Bunyan's nearly final comment is "Then I saw that there was a Way to Hell, even from the Gates of Heaven, as well as from the City of Destruction"!

The notion that professing believers can live and act as apostates with no danger to their eternal souls is a relatively new one. The Arminians, of course, have always maintained that Christians could lose their salvation whereas the prevailing position of the Reformers was that true believers, though they may backslide, would eventually repent and persevere in faith. But the idea that someone could believe for five or six months (or minutes, as some say), and then go back to atheism, immorality, and a life of sin, never to repent again, and still be saved, would have been inconceivable to both the original Reformers and Arminians!

More importantly, it really does seem to contradict Scripture. I know there are difficult passages. The warnings in Hebrews are particularly thorny, and I find myself not quite agreeing with the old Puritans or the Arminians on those. More on that later. But others are quite clear.

In the parable of the soils, Jesus says that only the seed that fell on "good soil" bore fruit. The path, the rock, and the thorns clearly represent three defective kinds of hearers: the devil stole the word from the first; persecution withered the word in the second, so that they deserted; and the riches, cares, and pleasures of the world choked out the word in the third, so that they failed to bear fruit. Certainly, we all display the attributes of these different soils at different times. But when someone's life as a whole is characterized by not hearing, not enduring, or not bearing fruit, isn't that the same as saying that they have, to use the words of James, "dead faith"?

Or take the apostle John's description of the apostates in his first letter: "They went out from us, but they were not of us; for if they had been of us, they would have continued with us. But they went out, that it might become plain that they all are not of us" (1 John 2:19). Perhaps more starkly, Peter describes the false prophets in his second letter as dogs returning to their vomit!

In each of these passages, it seems that the apostles are simply reiterating the teaching of our Lord: "You will recognize them by their fruits" (Matthew 7:16). These are not descriptions of regenerate believers who lost their salvation. They are descriptions of false professors who showed their true colors in the end. These passages warn us of the danger of a spurious, counterfeit faith.

Of course, this doesn't settle the vexing question of those warnings in Hebrews! And if I try to deal with those in this letter, I won't have time to answer your earlier question about the relationship between acedia and depression. So Hebrews will have to wait . . .

As for depression—yes, I do think there are sometimes physical causes for it. It's probably true that our culture as a whole runs to medication too quickly, but on the other hand, I have little patience with those Christians who judge people who use medication and quickly condemn the depressed for not having enough faith. Haven't these folks ever read the Psalms?

Whether your struggles with depression have physical as opposed to spiritual causes, I don't know and am in no position to answer. I'm neither a medical doctor, nor a trained psychologist. Just a pastor doing his best to deal with his own sins and shepherd the Lord's sheep. If the dark mood persists, I'd advise seeing a doctor. But even if biological factors contribute to your depression, I would encourage you to see the spiritual aspects for what they are as well. A healthier balance of work and rest as well as a steady diet of the Psalms would probably do you a lot of good. That said, judging from the relative absence of these emotions in the past (at least you never spoke of them last year when we were corresponding, nor in any of our face-to-face chats over the past few years), I suspect this is a season that will pass. Don't ignore it, though. Read your Psalms. Keep working. Get plenty of rest. And as soon as you settle in a church, share these burdens with a pastor who can both offer counsel and pray with you.

Can I leave you with yet another picture from Bunyan? (I told you I'd refer to him often). There's a scene when Christian and Hopeful get locked tight in Doubting Castle by a terrible monster called Giant Despair. There they languish for days as the dreadful giant returns again and again to mock them, beat them with his cudgel, and urge them to take their own lives. Do you know how they finally escape? It's only when Christian remembers the key in his bosom called Promise—a key that unfailingly opens every door in the castle. Don't lose your key, my friend!

Grace and peace,
Brian

Hope in God

Dear Chris,

I see that I've not been clear in the distinction I see between depression and acedia. In one of your letters, you described your condition as a "loss of interest in spiritual things," "laziness when it comes to prayer," and "a restlessness I'm finding hard to shake." My mind quickly went to acedia—partly, I confess, because I have struggled with this recently myself. But in another letter you described the "sadness that clings like a wet blanket," experiencing "refreshing rays of light" in worship even as you "feel the clouds come closing in again on Monday." You asked me if I thought "this depression" might have physical causes. And I said yes, it might, but that I couldn't be sure.

Now I find that I need to backtrack a little and make distinctions. In the original lists of deadly sins, despair (*tristitia*) and listlessness (*acedia*) were distinct from one another. Eventually, these two were combined in the one category of sloth. So while depression and acedia are related, they are not identical. The emotions one feels are much the same, but the causes are different, and the underlying orientations of the heart are different.

We should also further distinguish between various sorts of depression. There are physical factors, to be sure. Researchers, for example, have noticed that the hippocampus of the brain is smaller in people who suffer from clinical depression, which means that they have fewer serotonin receptors. Serotonin, as you may know, is a neurotransmitter that contributes to feelings of happiness and well-being. But the research, at least from what I've read, hasn't yet explained *why* some people have a smaller hippocampus. Again, I'm no scientist, but the data I've seen suggest that depression is a complex condition with many contributing factors.

Circumstances can also lead to depression: chronic illness, the death of a loved one, moving to a new place away from family and friends, and a hundred other sources of stress. All of these affect us physically, emotionally, and spiritually. I've personally faced this more in the past several years than I did in my twenties and early thirties, and I think the feelings have been at least partly related to several difficult circumstances I have experienced. My mother was diagnosed with a chronic and terminal illness. A number of people left the church I pastor to join a new church plant. And we've been in the throes of child rearing, with both the joy and exhaustion that comes with it. You've also faced some of these circumstantial difficulties, with the loss of a romantic relationship, the recent move to a new city, and being uprooted from your church family. I'm sure these things are all affecting you in one way or another.

But then there are the spiritual factors that can lead to depression: a sense of desertion by God, unanswered prayer, God's fatherly discipline when we have sinned, or oppression from dark spiritual forces (a reality we too often ignore). Psalms 42 and 43 give a fairly composite picture of such spiritual depression. From a careful reading of the two psalms (most scholars believe they were originally one), it's obvious that a whole collage of factors contributed to the writer being cast down in soul: (a) He suffered from insomnia and loss of appetite ("my tears have been my food day and night" in 42:3), (b) He was isolated from the worshiping community (42:4 suggests that he cannot worship in God's house), (c) He was taunted by enemies (see 42:3, 9 and 43:1–2), and (d) He felt abandoned by God (see 42:9).

Whether these are symptoms or causes, or some combination of both is hard to tell. What's clear is that these kinds of physical, circumstantial, and spiritual issues are at least often concurrent with depression. (Martyn Lloyd-Jones wrote an excellent book on this, by the way, called *Spiritual Depression: Its Causes and Its Cure*. You should pick it up. There's also an older Puritan volume by William Bridge called *A Lifting Up for the Downcast*. I've found each of these helpful during the darker seasons of my life.)

But we need to make a distinction here. While acedia may in many ways feel the same as depression, they are not the same thing. Sloth is one of the traditional seven deadly sins, but acedia isn't identical to sloth as we often think of it today—laziness when it comes to work or the proverbial couch potato ignoring responsibilities with eyes and heart glued to the tube. Though that's certainly sinful too, acedia can take a much more subtle form. Acedia is an indifference towards spiritual things, an inclination of the heart away from God, a laxness and laziness in using the means of grace. And it can mask itself in overwork, therefore not looking like sloth at all. Simply put, acedia is weariness with God.

Depression itself is not a sin. There are all sorts of reasons why a person may feel depressed, even while his or her heart is still fixed on God. Of course, we may also sin in the midst of depression, and no doubt we often do. At least I know that I have. But it's also possible for someone to be depressed (whether clinical depression or deep sadness about difficult circumstances or spiritual depression) and *not* be guilty of the vice of acedia. And it *is* a vice—not just a sin of which we are occasionally guilty, but a cultivated habit of the heart, a chosen path or way that is both wicked and destructive.

So here's the fundamental difference: acedia is a willful sin, while depression is a condition over which we have less control (I will not say we have none) and which we may experience even while our hearts are turned toward God.

Now, having made this distinction, I feel that I should backtrack yet more and say that perhaps I was too hasty in my diagnosis in your case. The Puritans thought of pastors as "Soul Physicians," and, unfortunately, just as MDs sometimes misdiagnose an initial presentation of symptoms, so do pastors. Your initial descriptions sounded more like acedia to me. But your recent letters indicate a heart that is fixed on the Lord, even though the darkness has not yet lifted.

Whatever the cause of your present distress, my sole desire is your well-being. Allow the Lord to search your heart for any vestiges of sin, and then follow the psalmist in preaching to yourself: "Why are you cast down, O my soul, and why are you in turmoil within me? Hope in God; for I shall again praise him, my salvation and my God" (Psalm 42:11).

In Christ alone,
Brian

The Danger of Apostasy

Dear Chris,

I'm glad that you're finding the Puritans, and especially Bunyan, helpful. It's always encouraging for me to see believers discover the older books for themselves. C. S. Lewis once wrote that "It is a good rule, after reading a new book, never to allow yourself another new one till you have read an old one in between." If that's too much, he said, at least read one old one to every three new ones! Of course, it's hard enough to find committed readers these days, though it seems that the advent of e-books may change that a little. In any case, I hope you enjoy reading *The Pilgrim's Progress* all the way through.

To answer your question, I do enjoy other kinds of books besides theology! In my leisure reading, I try to read both classic literature and biography, with an occasional splurge in popular fiction. Over the last year or so, for example, I've read several novels including Alan Paton's *Cry, The Beloved Country,* P. D. James' *The Children of Men,* Yann Martel's *Life of Pi,* and *The Hunger Games* trilogy. I've also read biographies on Theodore Roosevelt, Hudson Taylor, John Calvin, and John Wesley. I'm currently working on a biography of Augustine and Bronte's *Jane Eyre.* What else have you been reading? I'm always eager for suggestions.

About Hebrews: yes, chapters 6 and 10 are especially difficult, aren't they? I think I mentioned in an earlier letter that I don't find myself comfortable with either the Arminian line or the more traditional Calvinist reading. Of course, there are more than just these two views. Some interpreters think the warnings have more to do with the loss of rewards than with salvation. Others take a more hypothetical approach and think the warnings tell us what would happen if a believer failed to persevere, even as they insist that this is impossible. The traditional Reformed view, of course, essentially sees the warnings as tests that distinguish true believers from the false.

I suppose my position is something of an amalgam. It seems to me that far more is at stake than whether a believer will get certain rewards, while I also think there are good reasons for saying that a true believer cannot lose his or her salvation. On the other hand, it seems too simplistic to say that the warnings are merely tests of genuineness. I rather think that the warnings and admonitions are addressed to believers with a particular purpose in view—namely, to spur us onward in persevering faith. Think of them as the negative counterpart to God's promises. The promises of God assure us of God's covenant faithfulness, unfailing love, and sufficient grace, while the warnings evoke faith by showing us the real and eternal danger of turning away from Christ.

Think of it this way. If we take our children down to the river, we'll warn them not to get too close to the banks. It is dangerous, and the current could pull them under and drown them. When we say this, we do not mean to convince them that they are actually going to drown! Quite the opposite: we're warning them, because the warning is one way to protect them from the danger. We obviously keep a close eye on them so that their safety doesn't ultimately depend on their own watchfulness. But the warning still serves a function, and is based on the harsh realities that rivers are dangerous and people have drowned.

In the same way, Scripture warns believers of the dangers of apostasy. Unbelievers do perish. Falling away from Jesus is dangerous. There is no escape for those who turn away from such a great salvation (Hebrews 2:3). The balance of Scripture assures us that our Father holds his children so that they can never be snatched from his hand (John 10:29). Nevertheless, one of his means of keeping us is to warn us about the danger of falling away. Try reading the warnings in Hebrews through this lens and see if it doesn't make more sense than trying to argue that the warnings are written to expose false Christians.

One reason this paradigm makes more sense to me than the other views is because it accounts for the future, prospective nature of salvation. Many believers tend to collapse the biblical teaching about salvation into the single dimension of past conversion and justification. But Scripture presents salvation as a multi-dimensional reality with both present and future aspects. Yes, we have already been saved by grace through faith (Ephesians 2:8). But, on the other hand, "our salvation is nearer than when we first believed" (Romans 13:11) and those who have been justified by the blood of Christ "shall . . . be saved by him from the wrath of God" (Romans 5:9). So while it is true that we have already been saved in the past, it's also true that we shall be saved in the future. Salvation is already *and* not-yet. The kingdom has been inaugurated, but not yet consummated. We are justified, but not yet glorified. We are truly redeemed, but not fully redeemed.

If you want to study this subject further, Tom Schreiner and Ardel Caneday have co-authored a good book called *The Race Set Before Us: A Biblical Theology of Perseverance and Assurance*.

And in closing, let me say how grateful I am for the good report about the church. This is an answered prayer. I'm so glad to hear how you're feeding on the word and at the Table again.

Grace and peace,
Brian

The Price of Neglect

Dear Chris,

Sometimes I hardly know how to start a letter, so I just have to start writing. There seems to be no natural transition from my last letter to this one (and I've not received one from you in the past two weeks), but I find that I'm like the psalmist in that my heart grows hot within me, and when I muse, the fire burns. So I feel compelled to write—for my own benefit as much as, I hope, for yours.

My mind keeps returning to this ongoing discussion about acedia and depression. This morning I pulled John Cassian off my shelf, remembering that an entire book in his *Institutes* deals with *accidie*. He described it as "weariness or distress of heart" and said that it is "akin to dejection." But he still treated it as sinful, a peculiar temptation that "does not suffer [a monk] to stay in his cell, or to take any pains about reading." Cassian says it's like a battering ram that wears out the monk's wretched soul, so that he either sinks into slumber or seeks relief visiting some brother, only to be further weakened rather than helped. Eventually, the monk "begins to forget the object of his profession, which is nothing but meditation and contemplation of that divine purity . . . and so the soldier of Christ becomes a runaway from His service"—a deserter.

One of my first reactions is to think that the confines of a monastery would certainly produce such temptations! Who wants to spend their days cloistered from the rest of the world, denying the many good gifts God has given? Of course, many have pursued such a life in the hope of escaping the temptations of the world. But can we ever really do that? Our hearts want a thousand distractions even when none sit obvious before the eyes.

There are (it seems to me) defects in the whole monastic system. Remember that Paul warned against those who would "forbid marriage and require abstinence from foods that God created to be received with thanksgiving" and affirmed that "everything created by God is good, and nothing is to be rejected if it is received with thanksgiving, for it is made holy by the word of God and prayer" (1 Timothy 4:3–5). But Cassian's description of how acedia functions still rings true even if the circumstances within which he wrote were unbiblical in some respects. After all, I too have experienced this weariness and distress of heart that lays siege like a battering ram, forcing its way in to my soul, so that I'm tempted to slumber, sloth, and idle neglect.

Does this then call into question my earlier distinction between acedia and depression?

I said that acedia is a "willful sin," and I stand by that because I think acedia is a spiritual condition for which we are responsible. But "willful sin" can be misleading if you take it to mean a deliberately chosen sin—because acedia, in many ways, is more a sin of omission than commission. When Dante enters the fourth circle of hell he asks, "How is it that we choose to sin and wither?" and withering is a fitting metaphor for what happens to me when I languish in acedia's cold grasp. Like the cursed and barren fig tree in the Gospels, so my fruitless heart. But did I choose it?

Yes, but not directly. I chose it when I chose neglect.

Acedia, then, is that soul weariness that is the price of neglect. This isn't to say it causes all depression, but in some cases it does.

The warnings in Hebrews (yes, I am returning to those troublesome texts) seem targeted precisely at this. Have you ever noticed that there is a progression (or maybe regression) in the sins Hebrews warns against alongside a mounting urgency in the warnings themselves? In 2:1–4, the author warns against drifting from the gospel; in 3:8, 13–14 against hardening the heart; in 6:6 against falling way; in 10:26 against sinning deliberately; and in 12:25 against refusing to listen to Jesus' voice. This pattern displays the escalating tendency of sin. But it all starts with neglect, or drifting from the gospel.

Drifting from the gospel can begin in subtle, seemingly insignificant ways. Remember Screwtape's advice to Wormwood? "It does not matter how small the sins are provided that their cumulative effect is to edge the man away from the Light and out into the Nothing. Murder is no better than cards if cards can do the trick. Indeed the safest road to Hell is the gradual one—the gentle slope, soft underfoot, without sudden turnings, without milestones, without signposts."

I think that's why acedia is so dangerous. When a dark mood settles like thick fog in the soul, I'm confronted with a choice. I can either act against it or give in. Acting against it will take a myriad of forms like (in my case) saying my prayers, or preparing a sermon, or leading a meeting, or meeting with a parishioner, or washing the dishes, or mowing the yard. That is, acting against acedia often simply involves doing my daily tasks. On the other hand, giving in to acedia would mean avoiding those responsibilities and numbing out with too much television or food or Internet while leaving the mood itself unchecked. If I do that, then the fog settles, ennui moves in, and even my pleasure in God's good gifts begins to wane. Like a bad cold that robs one of taste, so acedia deadens the heart, making it feel impossible to taste and see that the Lord is good. (I say "feel impossible" because it's not *actually* impossible, but it does *feel* that way. Emotions can be terribly deceiving!) Dorothy Sayers described acedia as "the sin that believes in nothing, cares for nothing, seeks to know nothing, interferes with nothing, enjoys nothing, loves nothing, hates nothing, finds purpose in nothing, lives for nothing, and remains alive only because there is nothing it would die for."

I just remembered a scene from a book I read as a kid, Norton Juster's *The Phantom Tollbooth*. (Have you read it? It's quite good.) The protagonist, a little boy named Milo, finds himself driving through a rather dismal place:

> The sky became quite gray and, along with it, the whole countryside seemed to lose its color and assume the same monotonous tone. Everything was quiet, and even the air hung heavily. The birds sang only gray songs and the road wound back and forth in an endless series of climbing curves.
> Mile after
> mile after

mile after
mile he drove, and now, gradually, the car went slower and slower,
until it was hardly moving at all.

When Milo's car finally comes to a complete standstill, he is sur-
rounded by dull little creatures who blend into their surroundings
like chameleons taking on the color of whatever they happen to be
near. They are called the Lethargarians, and they quickly inform
him that it is against the law to laugh or think in the Doldrums.
"Well, if you can't laugh or think, what can you do?" asks Milo.
"Anything as long as it's nothing, and everything as long as it isn't
anything," they say.

It's a terrible place, and Milo is stuck there: his car will not move.
Can you guess how Milo finally gets out? By thinking!

> Milo began to think as hard as he could (which was very difficult,
> since he wasn't used to it). He thought of birds that swim and fish
> that fly. He thought of yesterday's lunch and tomorrow's dinner. He
> thought of words that began with J and numbers that end in 3. And,
> as he thought, the wheels began to turn. . . .
>
> The little car started to go faster and faster as Milo's brain whirled
> with activity, and down the road they went. In a few moments they
> were out of the Doldrums and back on the main highway.

There's much wisdom in that little book! And I will leave you with
that image as I've no more time to write: I have an elders' meeting
in an hour and must prepare. Do write again soon.

Brian

Is Salvation Unconditional?

Dear Chris,

I was glad to receive your thoughtful letter this afternoon. Thanks for your reflections on various books. Shared reading is one of the great delights of friendship, isn't it? By the way, have you read Alan Jacob's little book *The Pleasures of Reading in an Age of Distraction?* If not, get it—it's a real gem.

I hate to admit it, but I don't really like Dostoyevsky. I've read *Notes from Underground* and *The Brothers Karamazov,* and while I recognize the psychological depth of his characters and his brilliance in storytelling, I didn't deeply enjoy either book. Maybe you can persuade me to try him again, though.

Back to the questions of apostasy and assurance—you said something I resonate with and think is partly true, but without qualification I think it can be misleading and make some texts hard to handle. You said, "Salvation is unconditional," and I affirm this if you mean that justification is God's gift, freely bestowed on the undeserving, irrespective of our righteousness, merit, or works. *Sola gratia!* Amen!

But simply calling salvation "unconditional" isn't quite fine-grained enough. That statement presents two possible problems. First, we should not collapse the concept of salvation into the single category of justification. And second, Scripture uses conditional language for salvation, so we should as well.

As for justification—God's declaration that believing sinners are right with him through faith in Christ alone is indeed one of the most glorious realities of salvation. But it is a part, not the whole. The Bible uses multi-faceted language to describe salvation. There are the *legal* and *deliverance* metaphors conveyed with words like justification, forgiveness, and redemption. But there are also *family* metaphors (adoption, reconciliation, sonship), *renewal* metaphors (regeneration, creation, newness of life), and *cultic* metaphors (sanctification, holiness). We need to keep these many perspectives in mind when thinking about salvation as a whole, for while it is true that our effort plays no part in the legal aspects of salvation (justification), the same isn't true about sanctification or renewal. These are no less parts of salvation (when broadly, and biblically, considered) than justification and adoption. As I mentioned in an earlier letter, salvation in Scripture is multi-dimensional. It includes not only the past, but also the present and future. We *have been* saved, we *are being* saved, we *shall be* saved. (Again, see the book by Schreiner and Caneday if you want to read more. I have learned much from them.)

Let me also say more about the conditional language used in Scripture to describe salvation. Over and again, the promises of salvation are conditioned upon our response. Even justification, while not in any way based on our works, is still conditioned upon faith. Only those who believe are justified.

These conditions become even clearer when you notice how Scripture uses the word *if*. For example, in John 8, Jesus speaks to some who had "believed" in him, saying, "*If* you abide in my word, you are truly my disciples, and you will know the truth, and the truth will set you free" (verses 31–32). Do you see the condition? If they continue in Jesus' word, they are true disciples; if they do not continue, then they are not true disciples. The rest of the context makes clear that many of them had superficial faith, because Jesus tells them that they are the servants of sin (verses 34–35) and sons of the devil (verses 38–44), not of God (verse 47).

Consider another passage: "Now I would remind you, brothers, of the gospel I preached to you, which you received, in which you stand, and by which you are being saved, *if* you hold fast to the word I preached to you—unless you believed in vain" (1 Corinthians 15:1–2). Paul implies that though his readers had heard the gospel, received the gospel, and were presently standing in the gospel, they were only saved if they held fast to the same gospel. Failure to continue in the gospel would mean they had believed in vain. Some theologians say it doesn't matter if a person stops believing altogether because just one act of faith is sufficient to save. But that's not what Paul says.

He says it is possible to have believed the gospel in vain. Only those who keep believing are saved.

Here are more: We have been reconciled, "if indeed [we] continue in the faith, stable and steadfast, not shifting from the hope of the gospel" (Colossians 1:23). "We have come to share in Christ, if indeed we hold our original confidence firm to the end" (Hebrews 3:14). We will live, "if by the Spirit [we] put to death the deeds of the body" (Romans 8:13). And "If we confess our sins, [God] is faithful and just to forgive us our sins and to cleanse us from all unrighteousness" (1 John 1:9). The list could go on and on.

So what do all of these conditional statements imply? Do these verses mean that salvation is, after all, based on our works?

No.

Salvation isn't based upon our works because the same things Scripture represents as conditions are also gifts from God. As Augustine observed, God gives what he commands. Therefore, even our meeting of certain conditions is actually a gift of God's grace. Can a Christian be saved without perseverance in faith? No. But neither can a Christian persevere without God's grace enabling and guaranteeing his or her perseverance!

The conditions laid down in these "if" passages aren't meritorious works that we do to earn credit with God. They aren't conditions that we can fulfill in our own strength. Nor are they conditions that move us away from the gospel itself. In fact, all of the conditions boil down to one thing: continuing in the gospel. Persistent (not perfect) clinging to Jesus. Ongoing faith and repentance. Persevering in the obedience of faith. Holding fast the gospel.

But these are exactly the things that God gives. Faith is God's gift (Ephesians 2:8; Philippians 1:29; Acts 14:27; Hebrews 12:2). So is repentance (2 Timothy 2:25; Acts 11:18). And perseverance is not only our active continuance in faith and holiness, but also God's active preservation of our faith (Jude 24; 1 Peter 1:5; Philippians 2:13).

I think one of Augustus Toplady's old hymns says it best. The first verse reminds us that we are debtors to God's covenant mercy. It points us to our justification, for we wear Christ's righteousness and our transgressions are hidden by his obedience and blood. There is no condemnation in Christ!

> A debtor to mercy alone, of covenant mercy I sing;
> Nor fear, with thy righteousness on, my person and off'ring to
>   bring.
> The terrors of law and of God with me can have nothing to do;
> My Savior's obedience and blood hide all my transgressions
>   from view.

The second verse is about God's promise to finish what he started. Nothing can separate us from the love of Christ!

> The work which his goodness began, the arm of his strength
>   will complete;
> His promise is Yea and Amen, and never was forfeited yet.
> Things future, nor things that are now, nor all things below or
>   above,
> Can make him his purpose forgo, or sever my soul from his
>   love.

The third verse expresses the confidence that we, secure in God's love and grace, will endure to the end. We hold fast to him because he holds fast to us.

> My name from the palms of his hands eternity will not erase;
> Impressed on his heart it remains, in marks of indelible grace.
> Yes, I to the end shall endure, as sure as the earnest is giv'n;
> More happy, but not more secure, the glorified spirits in heav'n.

I hope this helps clarify things a bit. If you want to pursue this further, I recommend a wonderful section called "Unmerited, Conditional, Future Grace" in John Piper's book *Future Grace*. It's well worth studying.

A fellow debtor to mercy alone,
Brian

The Danger of Backsliding

Dear Chris,

You are definitely on the right track. Sometimes the first half of an "if/then" statement contains a certainty that guarantees the outcome. Take Romans 8:31, for example: "If God is for us, who can be against us?" Well, he *is* for us, so the answer is that no one can be against us!

Greek scholars call this a "first class condition." To put it simply, these kinds of conditional statements assume the reality of the premise for the sake of the argument. And when the premise is actually true, the conclusion that follows is sure. Other examples include 2 Corinthians 5:17 ("if anyone is in Christ, he is a new creation"), Romans 6:5 ("if we have been united with [Christ] in a death like his, we shall certainly be united with him in a resurrection like his"), and Colossians 3:1 ("If then you have been raised with Christ, seek the things that are above"). So yes, even the contingencies in Scripture can give hope.

On another note, it's interesting that you've been reading in Jeremiah. Have you thought about how relevant Jeremiah's overall message is to our discussion? Jeremiah was writing to a backslidden, apostate nation. (The KJV actually translates the Hebrew word for apostasy as *backsliding*.) And his imagery is piercing and provocative, picturing Judah's futile idolatry as prostitution and adultery of the worst sort. Jeremiah helps us see how serious sin really is.

For example, in chapter 2, Jeremiah pictures God's people as a bride who had once loved her husband (2:2) but who had now forsaken him (2:12–13). They were guilty of the most brazen harlotry. Jeremiah compares them to whores plying their trade under every tree in the land (2:20) and as restless camels and donkeys in heat, running to and fro in search of males (2:23–24). They are so far gone, in fact, that Jeremiah says *they* have taught the *prostitutes*! "Can a virgin forget her ornaments, or a bride her attire? Yet my people have forgotten me days without number. How well you direct your course to seek love! So that even to wicked women you have taught your ways" (2:32–33). The result of their adulterous idolatry was futility. They forsook God. Going far from him, they "went after worthlessness, and became worthless" (2:5) and "changed their glory for that which does not profit" (2:11). Following vain and empty delusions, they became vain, empty, and deluded themselves. They sought gods who couldn't satisfy (2:13) or save (2:27–28).

But even more interesting is how it happened. What led to Judah's apostasy? Why did the "honeymoon" (see 2:1–3) end, and why did they resort to such blatant idolatry? What was the cause of their backsliding?

It began with neglectful memory: "They did not say, 'Where is the Lord who brought us up from the land of Egypt, who led us in the wilderness' " (2:6). But who exactly forgot to call on the Lord? Four groups of leaders are indicted: the priests, those who handle the law, the shepherds, and the prophets (2:8). Those who should have pointed God's people to the Lord forgot him and forsook him themselves.

This is also the first step we take away from him. We forget. We fail to remember God's grace. We get gospel amnesia.

I think this especially shows up in our neglect of prayer and worship. In his heart-searching book on backsliding called *Personal Declension and Revival of Religion and the Soul*, Octavius Winslow said, "Thy sad distance from God is the secret of thy soul's leanness. The withering of the spirit of prayer has withered thy grace, and with it all spiritual enjoyment of the means. . . . All backsliding has its commencement in the declension of prayer."

There's a great illustration of this in C. S. Lewis's *The Silver Chair* (which is my favorite Narnian story, by the way). When Aslan gives Jill the lofty task of seeking and finding the lost prince of Narnia, he promises to give her four Signs. These Signs will guide her in the quest, but she *must* remember them:

"Remember, remember, remember the Signs. Say them to yourself when you wake in the morning and when you lie down at night, and when you awake in the middle of the night. And whatever strange things may happen to you, let nothing turn your mind from following the Signs…Remember the Signs and believe the Signs. Nothing else matters."

Jill begins well, of course, but she eventually quits repeating the Signs every night and forgets them. Then, in a critical moment, when Jill and her companions desperately need guidance, someone asks her if she is sure of the Signs. Annoyed by the question and miserably cold and tired, Jill retorts, "Oh come on! Bother the Signs." And the children end up in desperate trouble as they face giants, cannibals, and an evil Queen in the Underworld who tries to persuade them that "there is no Narnia, no Overworld, no sky, no sun, no Aslan."

We are too often like Jill ourselves. We neglect God, his word, and prayer, and then we find ourselves in dire straits where the enemy tries to persuade us that the realities of our faith are mere fables. When a wise and loving friend kindly asks, "How is your devotional life?" we lash out like Jill, "Oh come on! The Bible is irrelevant and prayer doesn't work! What's the use?" Maybe we don't say it out loud, but that's how we feel when we're trapped in the Underworld of unbelief. How desperately we need the sustaining, preserving grace of God!

Brian

Profile of an Apostate

Dear Chris,

The answer to your question is yes and no. Yes, I do believe that backsliding and sin pose a real danger to our souls. The warnings are genuine. But, no, I do not believe a born-again believer can completely fall away, and so fail in the end to be saved. Being foreknown, predestined, called, justified, and glorified, believers in Jesus are secure. Nothing can separate them from the love of Christ (Romans 8:29–39).

But assurance of salvation isn't like a birth certificate. You don't get it once, then file it away, only to pull out and use when doubts arise. The apostle Peter reminds us that only as we "supplement [our] faith" with virtue, knowledge, self-control, steadfastness, godliness, brotherly affection, and love will we "never fall." Conversely, he who lack these qualities is "blind, having forgotten that he was cleansed from his former sins." That's why he calls us to "make every effort" to grow and to "be all the more diligent to confirm your calling and election" (2 Peter 1:5–11).

This passage and many others teach us that the blessing of assurance depends on the ongoing exercise of faith. In the words of seventeenth-century Puritan pastor Thomas Brooks, "A lazy Christian shall always want [lack] four things: viz., comfort, content, confidence, and assurance. God hath made a separation between joy and idleness, between assurance and laziness; and, therefore, it is impossible for thee to bring these together that God hath put so far asunder."

This doesn't mean, of course, that we lose assurance every time we sin. What an intolerable emotional roller coaster that would be! As the old (and bad) joke goes, just as Calvinists have their TULIP, so Arminians also have a flower, the daisy: "he loves me, he loves me not, he loves me, he loves me not!" But God is not schizophrenic with his love. Neither must we be topsy-turvy in our assurance of his love.

This does mean, however, that we cannot persist in a course of unbelief and sin and continue to enjoy true assurance. (I stress "true" assurance, for just as there is counterfeit faith, so there is false assurance.) And further, since it is so difficult to tell the difference between a backsliding Christian (who is still "saved") and a false professor (who was never "saved" to start with), we can never allow ourselves to rest in a past experience of assurance apart from renewed faith and repentance.

That's another reason why I believe that both the warnings against apostasy and the sad examples of apostasy in Scripture have direct relevance to all confessing Christians. They show us the real danger in turning from Christ.

As a case in point, take the Old Testament character of King Saul recorded in 1 Samuel. Saul's story reads like a Shakespearean tragedy. He seems to start well, and the early chapters in 1 Samuel highlight his many attractive qualities: his physical stature (9:2; 10:23), humble attitude (9:21; 10:16, 22), spiritual power (10:9–10), political leadership (11:1–15), and military triumphs (14:47–48). But Saul's good start and many outward successes didn't guarantee a faithful finish.

So, what went wrong?

A. C. Bradley, the great Shakespeare scholar, observed that in almost all tragic characters, "we observe a marked one-sidedness, a predisposition in some particular direction . . . a fatal tendency to identify the whole being with one interest, object, passion, or habit of mind." As Bradley shows, you can certainly see this in Hamlet, Othello, Macbeth, and Lear.

But I think we also see in the narrative of 1 Samuel that something like a fatal flaw or a tragic trait emerges in Saul's character. The fatal flaw seems to be his desire to secure his kingdom at all costs. This leads him to offer an unlawful sacrifice (chapter 13), to make a rash vow (chapter 14), and to commit blatant disobedience (chapter 15). The kingdom is then torn away from him and given to another. From that time forward, his life spirals downward into self-destruction:

he descends into mental illness, jealousy, insanity, witchcraft, and eventually suicide on the battlefield.

The sad reality is that many people make choices and take paths that are just as tragic as Saul's. They start well but eventually allow sin to get the upper hand in their hearts as they increasingly harden themselves against God's grace.

There's a frightening scene in *The Pilgrim's Progress* where Christian encounters a man locked in an iron cage. When Christian asks how he came to be there, the despairing prisoner replies, "I left off to watch and be sober; I laid the reins upon the neck of my lusts; I sinned against the light of the word, and the goodness of God; I have grieved the Spirit, and He is gone; I tempted the devil, and he is come to me; I have provoked God to anger, and He has left me; I have so hardened my heart, that I cannot repent."

This is scary, but terribly serious. It is possible for us to so persistently harden our hearts to God's Spirit that we're eventually completely calcified in sin. In *The Great Divorce,* Lewis describes the damned as people with clenched fists and teeth, "their eyes fast shut. First they will not, in the end they cannot, open their hands for gifts, or their mouths for food, or their eyes to see."

And, were it not for grace, this is exactly what would happen to all of us.

This letter has admittedly focused on the dark side of this issue. There is, of course, much more to be said about grace and assurance. But this letter is already getting too long and I want to end on a practical point. What should you do when you realize you are on a bad trajectory? Hear the counsel of yet another great soul surgeon, John Owen. This is from his majestic exposition of Psalm 130 on the forgiveness of sins.

Are you in depths and doubts, staggering and uncertain, not knowing what is your condition, nor whether you have any interest in the forgiveness that is of God? Are you tossed up and down between hopes and fears, and want peace, consolation and establishment? Why lie you upon your faces? Get up: watch, pray, fast, meditate, offer violence to your lusts and corruptions; fear not, startle not at their crying to be spared; press unto the throne of grace by prayer, supplications, importunities, restless requests—this is the way to take the kingdom of God. These are not peace, are not assurance, but they are part of the means God hath appointed for the attainment of them.

I love that exhortation: "Get up: watch, pray, fast, meditate, offer violence to your lusts and corruptions." In short, use the means of grace to "press unto the throne of grace." Or, to return to Peter's words, "Give diligence to make your calling and election sure" (2 Peter 1:10, KJV).

With prayers,
Brian

The Divine Lover

Dear Chris,

No, you've got it all wrong! God isn't hovering over you with a "sledgehammer of judgment, waiting to pound you with wrath and condemnation." But I think I can see how my last letter may have left you with that impression. Maybe I should have counterbalanced the story of Saul and Bunyan's man in the iron cage with something more encouraging. Let me try again in this letter.

While Scripture certainly doesn't shrink away from the picture of God as righteous judge, this is balanced with the image of God as the grieving husband, desperately longing for his wayward wife to come home. Even with all the threats of judgment in the prophets, this is the dominant picture we get of God.

Don't forget that marriage is one of the metaphors Jeremiah uses to describe Yahweh's agonizing love for his people. Forgiveness is part of every good marriage, of course. But even so, we can barely fathom the soul-piercing beauty of God's covenant love. For Jeremiah pictures the Lord as the wounded, jilted lover, pursuing and pleading with his rebellious bride to return. The Lord makes this plea to return several times in Jeremiah 3: "'Return, faithless Israel,' declares the Lord, 'I will frown on you no longer, for I am faithful,' declares the Lord, 'I will not be angry forever'" (verse 12b) and "'Return, faithless people,' declares the Lord, 'for I am your husband'" (verse 14a) and "'Return, faithless people; I will cure you of backsliding'" (verse 22 NIV).

So there are three reasons why you should to turn back to God when you have backslidden: (1) He is faithful, and he will not be angry forever, (2) He is your husband, and he will restore you, and (3) He will cure, or heal, your backsliding. These are all pictures of grace: the lavish grace of a faithful and forgiving God, a husband who will restore us to himself, a physician who will give himself to heal us and to cure our spiritual decays and decline. I'm reminded of that hymn:

> O to grace how great a debtor
> Daily I'm constrained to be;
> Let thy goodness, like a fetter,
> Bind my wand'ring heart to thee.
>
> Prone to wander, Lord, I feel it,
> Prone to leave the God I love;
> Here's my heart, O take and seal it,
> Seal it for thy courts above.

I once saw an old film with Cary Grant, Deborah Kerr, and Robert Mitchum called *The Grass is Greener*. I don't particularly like the film, because it's about a British woman who contemplates adultery and decides to abandon her husband of many years for the charms of an American. Of course, the film is a comedy and it's all played up for laughs, taking the institution of marriage and the evil of adultery with far too little seriousness.

But in an interesting twist, the husband, Cary Grant, is desperate to woo her back and so challenges her potential lover, Robert Mitchum, to a duel. They will each fire pistols in this old-fashioned duel of honor. The wife, Deborah Kerr, protests all the way, and the American in no way wants to wound, much less kill, the husband. But what neither of them knows is that her husband has asked the butler to shoot him in the shoulder, giving him a non-lethal wound. He does this because he knows that being hurt in the duel will work on the sympathies of his wife and win her back. Sure enough, it works, and Cary Grant keeps his wife in the end.

There is nothing funny about adultery, much less spiritual adultery. But don't you see? God is the jilted lover, the loving husband who has been forsaken and spurned by his bride for other lovers. And he wins us back at the cross where God incarnate, Jesus Christ, died for the sake of his adulterous bride! It is seeing *this* that wins our affections back to him. He woos us by going to the ultimate limits:

sacrificing himself and dying as our substitute in our place. When we see his wounds, we are wooed to return.

> Then beneath the cross adoring,
> Sin does like itself appear;
> When, the wounds of Christ exploring,
> I can read my pardon there.

Before I end, one more quotation! I find these words from Ray Ortlund profoundly moving: "The biblical story lifts up before us a vision of God as our Lover. The gospel . . . sounds the voice of our Husband who has proven his love for us and who calls for our undivided love in return. The gospel reveals that, as we look out into the universe, ultimate reality is not cold, dark, blank space; ultimate reality is romance. There is a God above with love in his eyes for us and infinite joy to offer us, and he has set himself upon winning our hearts for himelf alone. The gospel tells the story of God's pursuing, faithful, wounded, angry, overruling, transforming, triumphant love. And it calls us to answer him with a love which cleanses our lives of all spiritual whoredom."

Brian

P.S. Thanks for the links to New Hope Covenant Church. Everything I've read looks good, and the sermons I've listened to were spiritually nourishing. Given everything you've said so far, I think you should join—and sooner, rather than later.

Intervening Grace

Dear Chris,

I didn't know you liked classical music! It's exciting how we keep discovering new overlapping interests. I grew up listening to classical music (no rock-n-roll in our conservative Baptist home!) and have always enjoyed it. My favorites are Tchaikovsky, Beethoven, Dvorak, and Mendelssohn. My most recent obsession has been Beethoven's symphonies. One of my new life goals is to attend a live performance of all nine of them. So far, I've only heard the Fifth, and what an experience!

Beyond classical music, I also enjoy (in spite of my upbringing!) rock (Coldplay, Mumford and Sons, U2), bluegrass (Allison Krauss), and occasional folk (Bob Dylan) or country (Johnny Cash). I started enjoying Johnny Cash after seeing the film *Walk the Line* several years ago and have been recently immersed in Cash's *American* recordings. I guess one reason I like the "man in black" is because his story is such a mix of faith and doubt, joy and pain, victory and defeat.

In his biography, *A Man Called Cash,* Steve Turner chronicled Cash's descent into a terrible drug addiction and the steps his family took to help bring him back. They first made plans to admit him to the Betty Ford Center and then set up an intervention: "In his private hospital room, his inner circle attempted to show him, in the clearest terms possible, the effect his selfish behavior was having on those he loved and who loved him. His wife, mother, and children all participated, each having written out a specific example of how his drugs had affected them." They told him how he was hurting them and had become distant to them. His personality had changed, and they could no longer meaningfully connect to him. They said they were worried about his health and feared that he would die. Their son, John Carter, expressed the humiliation he had felt in finding Cash stoned one day when he brought home a friend.

Turner says that "the challenging session ended with a simple statement from the doctor: 'We all want you to go to the Betty Ford Center.' Cash was humbled. He knew that the statements they'd read to him weren't written out of vengeance but out of love and concern. He agreed to go."

It has struck me that recovery from the downward spiral into sin follows a similar pattern. As Johnny Cash's family lovingly staged an intervention to rescue him from the precipice of destruction, so our God intervenes to rescue his people from our backsliding to the precipice of apostasy.

Effective interventions always have three components: confrontation (facing the problem), invitation (a plea to change), and direction (offering help and showing the path forward). We see each of those things in God's words to his wayward people through Jeremiah.

Rescue begins with *confrontation*, for there is no cure unless we face our sins. In Jeremiah 3:1–10 we see how God confronts sin. He doesn't only confront the sins themselves, but he also highlights the factors that aggravate sin and make it worse: the people's frequency in sinning (3:1–2), their boldness in sinning (3:3), and their pretense of repentance (3:10).

Do you see what God is doing? He is confronting his people with their sin. He's forcing them to face their true condition. This is the first step in intervening in order to restore them. Confrontation is a part of the process, because if we don't acknowledge that we have a problem, we can't be cured.

It's crucial for us to understand that when God confronts us, it is not for lack of love but *because* of love. Our culture tends to equate love with tolerance. Of course, it is not loving to behave in an ugly, condescending, or rude manner. But true love is *not* always tolerant. It isn't loving for a betrayed spouse to tolerate adultery. It's not loving for parents to tolerate lying and stealing by their children. It isn't loving for society to tolerate sexual abuse, rape, murder, or other violent crimes. And it wouldn't be loving for God to just give us a pass when we wander from his ways and drift away from him. As

Lewis wrote in *The Problem of Pain*, God "has paid us the intolerable compliment of loving us, in the deepest, most tragic, most inexorable sense"! And that means he must confront us when we sin.

The second step of intervention is *invitation*. In Jeremiah 3, God says, "Return," three times (verses 11, 14, and 22). The invitation is deeply practical in nature, as the Lord gives specific steps for restoration. The first step is confession: "Only acknowledge your guilt—you have rebelled against the Lord your God" (verse 13). Confession isn't simply verbal acknowledgement, of course. It's a brokenness over the evil in our hearts, which is why the Lord also says "break up your unplowed ground" (Jeremiah 4:3).

Confession must be joined with repentance:

> "If you, Israel, will return,
>   then return to me,"
>   declares the Lord.
> "If you put your detestable idols out of my sight
>   and no longer go astray,
> and if in a truthful, just and righteous way
>   you swear, 'As surely as the Lord lives,'
> then the nations will invoke blessings by him
>   and in him they will boast." (Jeremiah 4:1–2 NIV)

These verses show us that repentance involves returning to the Lord and removing our idols with a settled resolve to follow him. This is followed with covenant renewal (see the reference to circumcising the heart in Jeremiah 4:4). Circumcision was the outward sign and seal of inclusion in the Mosaic covenant, but it was also a symbol of the inward work needed in the heart (see Deuteronomy 30:6 and Romans 2:28–29).

Finally, God promises *direction* in the form of shepherds (Jeremiah 3:15–18). This reminds us that one of the ways God helps is through people, particularly people who can feed us with God's word and lead us in God's way. Call them pastors, shepherds, mentors, or spiritual directors—we all need them.

The church has recognized this for centuries, reaching back at least to Augustine who recorded in his *Confessions* how Ambrose helped him in his spiritual pilgrimage. We also see spiritual direction in the Protestant tradition. John Owen, for example, in his masterpiece on apostasy says that when backslidden believers have unsuccessfully "attempted their own deliverance," they should seek out "some able spiritual guide with their state and condition."

The ultimate Shepherd, of course, is Jesus who not only feeds and leads us but gives his life for the sheep. "I am the good shepherd. The good shepherd lays down his life for the sheep" (John 10:11). He is the Shepherd who gives us spiritual direction, who leads and feeds us with the food of his word, and who leads us back to the Father.

Now, back to Cash. In *Walk the Line*, the film made about his childhood and early career, young Johnny asks his older brother Jack how he can remember all the stories in the Bible. Jack responds, "You can't help people unless you tell them the right stories." So true. And the most powerful story of all is the story of God's grace in Jesus intervening to take the judgment we deserved so that we could be set free.

Cash believed and embraced this message, making both the gospel and his deep struggles with sin a centerpiece to much of his later music. On *American Recordings*, for example, he included a Romans 7-like ballad about his inner demons called "The Beast in Me." On *American IV: The Man Comes Around,* Cash covered the poignant song "Hurt" (written by Trent Reznor of Nine Inch Nails). Cash made the song his own and in the music video used a montage of images from his past that captured both his deep sense of regret and his reason for hope. The video was so moving that I cried the first time I saw it.

While those songs capture Cash's turmoil and struggle, they are balanced by others that exude deep, gospel hope. *American VI: Ain't No Grave* opens with the resurrection-themed title song, followed by "Redemption Day," and "1 Corinthians 15:55." But perhaps my favorite song from Cash is "Redemption," found on *American Recordings*, where he sings of the redeeming power of Jesus' blood, flowing down from his hands, side and feet, to bring him both freedom and life.

Cash understood that the cross of Christ is the only source of rescue from addiction. And so it is with us. His blood is the only effective cure for spiritual decline.

In Christ,
Brian

A Lifting Up for the Downcast

Dear Chris,

I was really moved by your humble confession in our phone call last night. The temptations you are facing are very difficult. I can only imagine the struggles you feel in wrestling with the hurt of rejection on one hand and the struggle for chastity on the other. It sounds like you've been fighting the sexual temptations with wisdom and perseverance. I don't want to minimize the conviction you've felt over your recent failures, but I do want to exhort you not to give way to discouragement and despair.

In my own struggles with sin over the years, I've found the counsel of William Bridge helpful over and again. Bridge wrote a little book for discouraged Christians called *A Lifting Up for the Downcast* (I think I've mentioned it before). It's been immensely helpful to me because he addresses different kinds of discouragement so specifically. For example, there are chapters to encourage those discouraged because of suffering and affliction, loss of assurance, a sense of desertion by God, temptation, "weak grace," "great sins," and more. Bridge takes every conceivable reason why a Christian may be discouraged and then skillfully applies the gospel to each case.

For example, while Bridge agrees that "the sins of God's own people do grieve the Spirit of God, are a dishonor to Jesus Christ, and do wound the name of God, and the profession of Christ," he insists that "saints have no reason to be discouraged or cast down." Why? Because saints know that "they shall never be condemned for their sin, whatever it be" (see Romans 8:1). Further, our sins can't separate us from God. Bridge is really helpful here: "Their sins may cause a strangeness between God and them, but shall never cause an enmity. Their sins may hide God's face from them, but shall never turn God's back upon them. Those whom God loves, he loves unto the end." And we shouldn't be discouraged, because "the overruling hand of grace" can turn even our sins into an "occasion of more grace and comfort. . . . God never permits his people to fall into any sin but He intends to make that sin an inlet into further grace and comfort for them."

Of course, there is an appropriate kind of sorrow that leads to repentance, but this is sorrow marked by humble trust in the Lord, not fearful and fretful discouragement or despair. Bridge helpfully distinguishes discouragement from being humbled: "When a man is humbled, truly humbled, the object of his grief or sorrow or trouble is sin itself, as a dishonor done unto God. The object of discouragement is a man's own condition."

Discouragement, in other words, is self-centered, rather than God-centered. And when we are focused on ourselves, we will lack joy. But "true humiliation is no enemy but a real friend unto spiritual joy, to our rejoicing in God. The more a man is humbled for sin committed, the more he will rejoice in God, and rejoice that he can grieve for sin." According to Bridge, this holds true, even in the case of great sins. We should always be humbled, but never discouraged. "A man is to be humbled for his sin, although it be never so small, but he is not to be discouraged for his sin, though it never be so great."

I think these distinctions are important and really just an application of Paul's distinction between godly and worldly sorrow in 2 Corinthians 7. The godly sorrow gives birth to repentance, while the sorrow of the world spawns death. And for myself, at least, I've learned that it's crucial for me to guard myself from the latter. It's easy for us to get discouraged about our sins, while not really being repentant at all. Discouragement is often just the flipside of self-confidence. I recall reading somewhere that "to be disappointed in yourself is to have believed in yourself." Guard against that kind of discouragement, brother. Repent, turn to Christ, rest in his forgiveness and mercy, and resume walking with God.

I'll leave you with a helpful illustration from Bridge. He contrasts two ways of putting out a candle. One person blows the candle out but finds it is easily lighted again. The other puts the candle in the water, making it much harder to reignite. "Likewise," Bridge says, "temptations blown out with resolutions and moral reasons easily return, but quenched in Christ's blood do not."

So, dear friend, quench your temptations in the blood of our Savior that cleanses us from sin. Be vigilant and watchful against sin, but don't trust in your new resolutions. Stay close to Jesus himself.

Brian

The Wounded Surgeon

Dear Chris,

Your self-description in your last letter was spot-on, not just as a diagnosis of your own heart but of the human condition as a whole. All of us, not just you, are "ridden with the disease of sin, in desperate need of the Divine Physician's healing touch." Scripture often uses sickness as a picture of sin. Isaiah's verdict of Israel applies to us all: "The whole head is sick, and the whole heart faint. From the sole of the foot even to the head, there is no soundness in it, but bruises and sores and raw wounds" (Isaiah 1:5b–6).

This suggests yet another metaphor for the Christian life—that of gradual restoration to health. Our souls are sick with sin, but God restores us to health through his healing, saving word. Jesus himself pictured sin as a disease when he said, "Those who are well have no need of a physician, but those who are sick. I came not to call the righteous, but sinners" (Mark 2:17).

I also think we're warranted to view the healing miracles of Jesus in the Gospels not just as historical records of true healings of genuine physical deformities and diseases but as signs of something even more significant. As Pascal observed,

> The figure used in the Gospel for the state of the soul that is sick is that of sick bodies. But, because one body cannot be sick enough to express it properly, there had to be more than one. Thus we find the deaf man, the dumb man, the blind man, the paralytic, dead Lazarus, the man possessed of a devil. All these put together are in the sick soul.

The sickness of sin is graphically described in Psalm 107, which pictures some who "were fools through their sinful ways and because of their iniquities suffered affliction," who thus "loathed any kind of food" and "drew near to the gates of death" (verses 17–18). It's a vivid picture of someone dying from a wasting disease, right on the edge of death. You can imagine the body emaciated and frail, the face ashen white, the brow burning with fever. And the most telling symptom of all: the total loss of appetite. That's what the disease of sin does. It steals our health, robs us of our life, and ruins our appetite for the good.

But thank God the psalm doesn't end there! "Then they cried to the Lord in their trouble, and he delivered them from their distress. He sent out his word and healed them, and delivered them from their destruction" (verses 19–20). Those verses show us both the condition for healing and its source. The condition is honestly crying out to God. Like blind Bartimaeus of Jericho, we must cry out, "Jesus, Son of David, have mercy on me!" (Mark 10:47).

The source of healing is God's saving word. Of course, this points us to God's spoken and written word, which is both a scalpel to remove the cancer of sin (Hebrews 4:12) and the food our spirits need, providing nourishment which nurses back to health (Deuteronomy 8:3). But the word of God in Scripture is not only his spoken and written word, but also the living word, the Word made flesh (John 1:14). And it is only through Christ, the living word, that we can be healed. In fact, Jesus said that Scripture itself pointed to him, and he rebuked those who missed the Word in the word when he said, "You search the Scriptures because you think that in them you have eternal life; and it is they that bear witness about me, yet you refuse to come to me that you may have life" (John 5:39–40). For the Word is not just a medicine, it is a Person—a Physician who comes to heal us. And how does he heal us? By dying for us.

In his *Four Quartets*, T. S. Eliot speaks of the "wounded surgeon" who heals us:

> The wounded surgeon plies the steel
> That questions the distempered part;
> Beneath the bleeding hands we feel
> The sharp compassion of the healer's art
> Resolving the enigma of the fever chart.

But then he tells us how that "wounded surgeon" accomplishes total healing for his patients:

> The dripping blood our only drink,
> The bloody flesh our only food:
> In spite of which we like to think
> That we are sound, substantial flesh and blood—
> Again, in spite of that, we call this Friday good.

How are we healed? By the bleeding hands of our wounded surgeon. By his sharp compassion that sent him to the cross—the cross that shows us we are *not* sound, we are *not* healthy. The cross resolves "the enigma of the fever chart," telling us how sick we really are, how our sins are great enough to crucify the Son of God. But the cross also points us to his "dripping blood" and "bloody flesh" as our drink and food, so that in the end, "we call this Friday good." Why do we call it good? Because "by his stripes we are healed."

So, once again, take heart and do not focus on your progress or lack thereof, but on Christ himself and the certainty of his promise to lead you all the way home. As Luther said, "This life . . . is not righteousness but growth in righteousness, not health but healing, not being but becoming, not rest but exercise; we are not yet what we shall be, but we are growing toward it." Though you are still troubled with the smarting pain of your wounds, you are in convalescence. Soon, you'll be whole again.

Hoping in the gospel,
Brian

The Good Fight of Faith

Dear Chris,

What you are facing is normal. Milestone spiritual experiences are almost always followed by seasons of intensified conflict and battle. Remember that Jesus was tempted in the wilderness right after his baptism. You can be sure that the "ancient serpent" (Revelation 12:9) is poised to strike when you're least expecting it.

This underscores the need to be both well prepared and watchful. I think we seriously underestimate what it means to count the cost in following Jesus (Luke 14). I recall an old preacher who used to say, "The more you sweat in training, the less you bleed in battle." But where is the sweat in our discipleship today?

One of my favorite essayists, Annie Dillard, tells the fascinating story of John Franklin leading a British Arctic expedition intending to chart the Northwest Passage. Two ships with 138 men set out on the journey. But no one survived or returned. The fault was in the preparation. Franklin failed to realize the danger of their venture and loaded his ships with a 1,200-volume library, ornate china place settings and silverware, and a hand organ. The crew was also ill-equipped. Not anticipating the extreme Arctic temperatures, they packed only their Navy-issue uniforms and a 12-day supply of coal for their auxiliary steam engines. And for a two- to three-year voyage! (I feel like my family takes more on our annual trips to Georgia and Texas!) When the ships sailed into frigid waters, they were quickly trapped in ice. The expedition was doomed. Though the sailors searched for help, the severe temperatures beat them. Every man among them died.

So many people approach Christianity the same way. They fail to assess the danger, count the cost, and adequately prepare for the arduous and grueling journey ahead. Our fallen world isn't friendly to faith; it's hostile enemy territory where we're assaulted by foes on every side. As someone once said, "The Christian life is not a playground; it is a battleground," and it demands constant vigilance, persevering holiness, and lifelong endurance.

That's why one of the most frequent biblical metaphors for the Christian life is a fight. Paul says we are to "fight the good fight of the faith" (1 Timothy 6:12) and "Share in suffering as a good soldier of Christ Jesus" (2 Timothy 2:3). Jesus warned his disciples to "Watch and pray" (Matthew 26:41), and 1 Corinthians 16:13 tells us to "Be watchful, stand firm in the faith, act like men, be strong." Then there is Paul's more detailed instructions about the Christian's battle, enemy, and armor in Ephesians 6. "True Christianity is a struggle, a fight and a warfare. . . . Where there is grace there will be conflict. The believer is a soldier. There is no holiness without a warfare. Saved souls will always be found to have fought a fight," wrote J. C. Ryle in his classic work on holiness.

Simply put, we're at war. As soldiers of Christ, we contend with our own sinful flesh as well as Satan, the great enemy of our souls. "Your adversary the devil prowls around like a roaring lion, seeking someone to devour" (1 Peter 5:8). He will cross our intentions to follow Jesus at every turn. In Luther's familiar words:

> For still our ancient foe
> Doth seek to work us woe;
> His craft and pow'r are great
> And, armed with cruel hate,
> On earth is not his equal.

The battle is fierce, and though God's saving plan can't be thwarted, we won't stand in victory over the enemy unless we appropriate God's all-sufficient grace for the fight. We must "stand *against* the schemes of the devil." We wrestle "*against* the rulers." We wrestle "*against* the authorities." We wrestle "*against* the cosmic powers over this present darkness." We wrestle "*against* the spiritual forces of evil in the heavenly places" (Ephesians 6:11–12).

Against, against, against, against, against! Paul uses this word six times in two verses! Make no mistake, brother: we have a world of evil against us!

Imagine yourself as a foot soldier. You are on an ongoing journey back to your base camp, where you will be welcomed by the general, treated for your wounds, rewarded for your conquests, and returned to your country. But between you and the base camp are three hundred miles of enemy territory and you can't advance a single inch without being shot at.

Paul writes with that kind of urgency. I can't live one day without danger. Every time I read my Bible, evil is at my elbow. I can't get on my knees to pray without the devil tickling my ear with his whispering wiles. I can't grow in grace, pursue holiness, show love, mortify sin, or worship God without potentially being assaulted. It's an intense fight. But the Lord has provided us with what we need to fight this war. To quote Luther again,

> The Spirit and the gifts are ours
> Through him who with us sideth.

So, what is our hope? Only Christ. "Be strong *in the Lord* and the power of *his* might. Put on the whole armor of God" (Ephesians 6:10). Paul's words slay self-sufficiency. This isn't a call to muster up our own energy for the battle but a reminder to depend on the strength of our Brother, Captain, and King. Don't think you can win these battles against lust and discouragement on your own. You can't. Victory will only come as you lean on Jesus. Luther once more:

> Did we in our own strength confide,
> Our striving would be losing;
> Were not the right man on our side,
> The man of God's own choosing.
> You ask who that may be?
>   Christ Jesus, it is he,
> Lord Sabaoth his name,

> From age to age the same,
> And he must win the battle.

Amen! That's a good place to end. Let's talk on the phone after Sunday. In the meantime, you remain in my prayers.

In the trenches with you,
Brian

Put on the Gospel Armor

Dear Chris,

Rather than writing in detail about each piece of armor in Ephesians 6, let me recommend a couple of good resources for you and then make a few general observations about the armor that I think are easily overlooked or forgotten.

Of course, I'm thrilled that you're taking the fight so seriously. And you are right to want to understand this passage as fully as possible. So, first, the recommendations. The best overall commentary on Ephesians is by Peter O'Brien. It's on the technical side but still suitable for the educated layperson. I think you'll like it. For sermons, check out Martyn Lloyd-Jones. And if you want to dig into the most thorough application of the armor, get William Gurnall's *The Christian in Complete Armor.* I confess, I've never read it all the way through, but I always benefit from dipping into it.

Now, my general observations.

This is God's armor. Why is it called "the armor of God"? In part, because God has provided it. He is the one who supplies it for us. And in light of the rich echoes of Isaiah 59 in this passage, it's also true to say that this is God's *own* armor.

Here's the background. In Isaiah 59:12–16, the prophet visualizes the dire condition of God's people and the casualties of justice, righteousness, truth, and uprightness, such that the only solution is for God himself to come and battle for his people. Then in verse 17, he says that the Lord "put on righteousness as a breastplate, and a helmet of salvation on his head; he put on garments of vengeance for clothing, and wrapped himself in zeal as a cloak." So the breastplate of righteousness and the helmet of salvation are clearly God's own! Just as a king might give his own sword and lend his own steed to his favored knight before battle, so God resources the church with his very own strength and power.

Why is that significant? Because it reminds us that our armor—our defense against the enemy—is divine in origin and supernatural in character. And it shows us that the armor is an armor of virtue, of godliness, of holiness. It is not some mystical thing that we gain in addition to a holy life—it is holiness and godly character itself. "For though we walk in the flesh, we are not waging war according to the flesh. For the weapons of our warfare are not of the flesh but have divine power to destroy strongholds" (2 Corinthians 10:3–4a).

This armor is complete. Paul says to put on and take up "the whole armor of God" (Ephesians 6:11, 13). Actually the word *whole* is not in Greek, but it is implied in the word for armor—the word *panoplia*, from which we get our word *panoply*, which is another word for armor. But one scholar points out that this "is the term used for the full equipment, both defensive and offensive, of the heavily armed foot soldier." This means that we are fully armed.

Of course, the belt, breastplate, shoes, shield, helmet, and sword are metaphors. Paul simply uses this vivid imagery to describe the complete panoply of virtues with which a Christian must be armed: truth (or truthfulness), righteousness, the gospel of peace, faith, salvation, the word of God, and prayer. Paul's use of the metaphor of the complete armor shows us the sufficiency of God's strength and grace for our warfare. God "has granted to us all things that pertain to life and godliness" (2 Peter 1:3).

The armor must be put on! We must appropriate the gospel to our lives. We must apply the truth God has given. As Gurnall said, "It is not enough to have grace, but this grace must be kept in exercise. The Christian's armor is made to be worn; no laying down, or putting off our armor, till we have done our warfare, and finished our course."

This also means we can't pick and choose which pieces we are going to wear. A soldier doesn't choose to wear part of the uniform or carry certain select weapons. He carries all that is regimented. He is entirely equipped. No cafeteria-style obedience. We can't say, "Oh, I've got truthfulness and I'm sincere, so it doesn't matter if I don't have righteousness or if I'm not holy." We can't say, "Hey, I have the word of God, so what does it matter if I pray or not?" Or, "I'm a prayer-oriented person, but I don't like to read, so I just don't get into Bible study." Or, "I'm saved—I've got salvation, so what does it matter whether I'm living right?" We must never put asunder what God has joined together!

The armor is necessary for victory. Paul gives basically the same command twice in two verses very close together: "Put on the whole armor of God, that you may be able to stand against the schemes of the devil" (Ephesians 6:11), and then "Therefore take up the whole armor of God, that you may be able to withstand in the evil day, and having done all, to stand firm" (Ephesians 6:13). I think he repeats himself because the armor is essential for victory. You cannot stand without the armor. Notice verse 13: "and having done all, to stand firm." You must have done *all*—you must have fully appropriated the armor if you are going to stand.

When Paul got to the end of his life, he was still standing. He had fought the good fight, finished the race, and kept the faith (2 Timothy 4:7). That prompts me to ask, "Will you be standing at the end? Will I?" As I enter into middle age, I feel more urgency about this because I know people who started well but who are no longer standing. A mentor who lost his ministry through emotional infidelity. A professor who left his wife for a younger woman. A deacon who embezzled thousands of dollars from his employer.

That's one reason why I'm so keen to keep this correspondence up. Because I want to see you standing ten years from now. So keep learning. Keep studying. Keep praying. Keep pursuing purity. And, as the old hymn says,

> Put on the gospel armor
> Each piece put on with prayer.

Stay in the fight, brother!
Brian

Rightly Ordered Loves

Dear Chris,

You've hit on one of the perennial challenges of the Christian life! How do you live in the world without idolizing it on the one hand, or wrongly denying its goodness on the other? Individual believers, and even whole movements within Christendom, tend to fall off one precipice or the other. Some aspects of Fundamentalism prioritized separation from the world to the point that they spurned secular music, movie theaters, and certain forms of dress *in toto*. Contemporary evangelicals, on the other hand, sometimes not only tolerate, but also embrace aspects of the world that would have made our forefathers blush with shame. Some of these differences are cultural, but certainly not all. I'm not a teetotaler, nor do I see anything inherently wrong with watching movies or wearing shorts. Total avoidance of the world is impossible, and those who attempt it often screen out the gnats of entertainment while swallowing the camels of self-righteousness and pride.

But that doesn't mean there are no dangers in the world! My heart is prone to wander. To borrow from Calvin, it's an idol factory. The problem is that I can idolize not just the bad things, but also the good. We could even say that every evil thing really is a good thing corrupted by inordinate love.

This line of thought isn't original with me, of course. C. S. Lewis discusses it in his essay "First and Second Things" in this way: "Every preference of a small good to a great, or a partial good to a total good, involves the loss of the small or partial good for which the sacrifice was made. Apparently the world was made that way. . . . You can't get second things by putting them first; you can get second things only by putting first things first." And in one of his letters, Lewis said that sensual love "ceases to be a devil when it ceases to be a god," for a *real* thing "is good if only it will be humble and ordinate."

Those statements contain a wealth of insight about the nature of sin. Sin isn't simply doing bad deeds. Sin is making a good thing into an ultimate thing, thus displacing God himself as first and best. Sin, at its heart, is idolatry: what Don Carson calls "the de-godding of God." When God isn't the center of gravity in my universe, then all the other pieces begin to stray like planets out of orbit. But when God is central, every other good takes its proper place in relationship to him.

The battle, then, isn't so much to separate from the world *per se*. It's rather to keep the world, and all worldly goods, in their proper—humble and ordinate—place. This is what Saint Augustine described as the right ordering of our loves. "Living a just and holy life," he said, "requires one to be capable of an objective and impartial evaluation of things: to love things, that is to say, in the right order, so that you do not love what is not to be loved, or fail to love what is to be loved, or have a greater love for what should be loved less, or an equal love for things that should be loved less or more, or a lesser or greater love for things that should be loved equally."

I think this is what the apostle Paul was getting at when he said, "let those who have wives live as though they had none, and those who mourn as though they were not mourning, and those who rejoice as though they were not rejoicing, and those who buy as though they had no goods, and those who deal with the world as though they had no dealings with it. For the present form of this world is passing away" (1 Corinthians 7:29b–31). We are involved in the world (marriage, grief, joy, possessions, etc.), but our involvement should be free of undue attachment.

At first, this may sound more ascetic than it really is. Paul obviously doesn't mean that spouses shouldn't love their mates (remember, he's primarily talking about marriage in the above passage); in fact, he commands this elsewhere. Instead, he means that they shouldn't make such love primary. Marital love is good when it is humble and ordinate. As is a career, possessions, food and drink, and any other number of things. But if you put any one of these first, making it the central and primary thing in your life, it will destroy you. Food is good, gluttony is destructive. Wine is good, drunkenness is destructive. Rest is good, sloth is destructive. Money is good, greed is destructive. Sex in marriage is good, sex outside of marriage is destructive.

This is why Augustine defines virtue as rightly ordered love and prays,

> These are thy gifts; they are good, for thou in thy
> goodness has made them.
> Nothing in them is from us, save for sin when,
> neglectful of order,
> We fix our love on the creature, instead of on thee,
> the Creator.

Lewis, once more, provides the best picture of what I mean. In *Prince Caspian*, one of the Narnia books, Aslan is conspicuously absent for much of the story. The children have come to a Narnia that has sadly forgotten the beauty, magic, and joy of Aslan's reign. The mythical creatures and Talking Beasts are in hiding, and the Telmarines reign instead.

When Aslan finally returns, he brings the beauty and magic back with him, restoring joy to Narnia. And following Aslan comes Bacchus, the mythical Roman god of wine, along with his tutor Silenus, accompanied by a consort of centaurs, dryads, and satyrs, who come in dancing wildly around the lion. Trees come to life, a river-god is awakened, the peoples of Narnia drink wine and feast sumptuously, children escape boring and untrue history classes— wonder and joy have returned!

But near the end of chapter 11, Susan says, "I wouldn't have felt very safe with Bacchus and all his wild girls if we'd met them without Aslan."

Here's the point. All created things are good as long as they take their rightful place under the reign of Jesus in the kingdom of God. As one of Lewis's Bright Spirits says in *The Great Divorce*, "No natural feelings are high or low, holy or unholy in themselves. They are all holy when God's hand is on the rein. They all go bad when they set up on their own and make themselves into false gods."

So how can I keep my loves humble and ordinate? By keeping them under Jesus. Only when he holds the reins of all my ambitions and desires, loves and relationships, joys and sorrows, cares and concerns am I safe from the danger of idolatry—from losing both the sweet sense of his presence and the true unalloyed blessing that he intends to give in all other goods.

I really believe that is the key. But how often I've failed and allowed some other *lesser* thing to creep its way into my affections and cast a shadow between Jesus and me! If it were not for grace, I'd be undone.

Brian

P.S. I just remembered one more Lewis reference that relates to this. Remember how Screwtape encourages Wormwood to use dullness as a temptation to abuse proper pleasures? I think it's in the ninth letter. Good reminder of our need to "watch and pray," especially during seasons of weariness, dryness, and discouragement.

Enjoying God in Everything

Dear Chris,

I got your email this morning just after arriving at the local coffee shop. Nothing like leisurely reading over fresh coffee on a day off! I've been working through Peter Brown's biography on Augustine and came across a fascinating quote from *The City of God* that may help clarify what I was trying to say in my last letter. In thinking about the entrancing sight of the water off the Bay of Hippo, Augustine wrote, "There is a grandeur of the spectacle of the sea itself, as it slips on and off its many colors like robes, and now is all shades of green, now purple, now sky blue, and all these are mere consolations for us unhappy, punished men, they are not the rewards of the blessed. What can [the rewards of the blessed] be like, then, if such things here are so many, so great, and of such a quality?"

Do you see what Augustine has done? He has not rejected the grandeur of the sea with its mesmerizing kaleidoscope of colors; he has rather received this created good as a pointer to the Ultimate Good, God himself. This is exactly what C. S. Lewis teaches us to do when he says that we should "make every pleasure into a channel of adoration." After all, "pleasures are shafts of the glory as it strikes our sensibility." But when we experience any pleasure, we find that it isn't ultimate, but rather points to that which is ultimate. "This heavenly fruit is instantly redolent of the orchard where it grew. This sweet air whispers of the country from whence it blows. It is a message. We know we are being touched by a finger of that right hand at which there are pleasures for evermore."

If we'll only be attentive, we will experience such pleasures in myriads of ways. While walking along a path strewn with the golden leaves of the forest woods. Or listening to Beethoven's Seventh symphony. Or reading Tolkien's lyrical prose in *The Lord of the Rings*.

We hear these whispers when watching beautiful films (such as my most recent favorite, Terrence Malick's *The Tree of Life*). We taste this heavenly fruit when savoring conversation with a close friend over a glass of fine wine. We catch a dim glimpse of this Joy in the sheer delight writ full on the face of a child. In any and all of these moments, we can feel the faint touch of his hand.

Our response in these moments should be twofold. On one hand, we should be grateful. "Thank you, God, for this!" But, like Augustine, we should then move from gratitude to adoration. In Lewis's words, "Adoration says, 'What must be the quality of that Being whose far-off and momentary coruscations are like this!' One's mind runs back up the sunbeam to the sun."

This not only gives us a way to enjoy pleasures without committing idolatry, but as we learn how to enjoy God in everything, we cultivate hearts full of worship. Here's how Lewis describes it:

> One must learn to walk before one can run. So here. We . . . shall not be able to adore God on the highest occasions if we have learned no habit of doing so on the lowest. At best, our faith and reason will tell us that He is adorable, but we shall not have *found* Him so, not have "tasted and seen." Any patch of sunlight in a wood will show you something about the sun which you could never get from reading books on astronomy. These pure and spontaneous pleasures are "patches of Godlight" in the woods of our experience.

This is what you are learning to do, my friend. You've tasted and seen that the Lord is good. And now you are learning to trace the sunbeam back to the sun: to enjoy God in all your other enjoyments, to love God in all your loves.

George Herbert expressed this beautifully in his great poem "The Elixir."

> Teach me, my God and King,
>   In all things Thee to see,
> And what I do in anything,
>   To do it all for Thee

And the last stanza . . .

> This is the famous stone
>   That turneth all to gold;
>   For that which God doth touch and own
>   Cannot for less be told.

As you probably know, in mythology an elixir is a stone that converts base metals into gold. Herbert sees the life devoted to pleasing God as having a similar power: it transforms everything into worship.

Indulge me one more quotation before I sign off and go back to Augustine. This one is from Jonathan Edwards, who reminds us that even our best pleasures here are still small in comparison to the "solid joys and lasting pleasures" found in God himself. Edwards said,

> The enjoyment of [God] is the only happiness with which our souls can be satisfied. To go to heaven, to fully enjoy God, is *infinitely* better than the most pleasant accommodations here. Fathers and mothers, husbands, wives, or children, or the company of earthly friends, are but shadows; but the enjoyment of God is the substance. These are but scattered beams; but God is the sun. These are but streams; but God is the fountain. These are but drops; but God is the ocean.

Joyfully,
Brian

Spiritual Blahs

Dear Chris,

How are you, my friend? It's been a couple of months since I've heard from you, so I thought I would write.

Did I mention that I am writing a book? Well, trying to anyway. It's abominably hard work and sometimes half the day drains away in a slow trickle of fruitless, seemingly wasted effort composing the same lame paragraph again and again and again.

Today has been such a day. So, if you'll pardon both my mood and my motive, I'm writing you instead. At least this has the virtue of not having to survive an editor's surgical eye!

Just prior to starting this letter I reread Anne Lamott's chapter on writer's block in her winsome little book on writing. One thing she said stuck. She said that she no longer thinks of this experience as block: "I think that is looking at the problem from the wrong angle. If your wife locks you out of the house, you don't have a problem with the door. The word *block* suggests that you are constipated or stuck, when the truth is that you're empty."

The remedy, of course, is to stop trying to force genius (I've tried, and it can't be done) and to focus instead on filling up one's mind and heart. When the car is out of gas, it does no good to push. The only way to get up to speed again is to fill the tank.

I bring all this up because (1) It's on my mind, and in writing you, I'm at least writing *something*, and (2) I think this is a useful parable for the spiritual life. Sometimes we feel something akin to writer's block in our spiritual lives. We find that we can't pray or worship or meditate. The mind is blank, the heart is dull, the soul is dim. Sharing your faith with someone else feels like trying to dismantle a skyscraper with a screwdriver.

I know there are some pious souls who never seem to experience anything like this inertia I've described. Whether they are hypocrites or lacking in self-awareness or far more spiritually advanced than I is for someone else to say. That I find them so irritating is no doubt a defect in my own character.

The question is what shall we do with these spiritual blahs? The answer, of course, is that we must refuel. Fill up the inner place. But how to do that? Well, I suppose there are as many possible answers as there are people. Different strokes for different folks, right?

For myself, it requires intentionally refueling every empty tank. Rest for the body. Learning for the mind. And some kind of aesthetic stimulation for the imagination (walking the beach, reading good literature, listening to a symphony).

It occurs to me that worship services, when planned well, often contribute to this restoration of soul. As a pastor, I am seldom exposed to worship outside of our own church. But from the reports I hear, far too much worship in the contemporary church is bereft of the very elements most conducive to spiritual restoration. The entertainment so common in megachurches won't do it—there's not enough substance to deeply challenge the mind or enough beauty to experience transcendence. But I think the more traditional fare in many smaller churches also fails to cut the mustard. What we need is a combination of intentionality in crafting a service that is rich in biblical/theological content with earnest pleading for the Spirit's powerful presence. I'm convicted as I write—surely we need more of this in our church, especially the earnest pleading!

Well, please forgive my rather grumpy rambling. An hour has passed since I began this letter and it's time for dinner with Holly and the kids, so I must go. Do write again soon and please pray for me as I do for you.

Brian

The Proper End and Design of Evangelical Truths

Dear Chris,

Thanks for your encouraging note about my writing. Sometimes when I sit down to work on the book, I remember how Flannery O'Connor called one of her novels "Opus Nauseous No. 1." I know how she felt, and the sad reality is that my best writing will pale in comparison with her worst. But how irksome of me to respond to your sincere encouragement like this. I meant to thank you, but now I'm becoming myopic again.

One of the most important writers for my spiritual growth has been the seventeenth-century theologian John Owen. I'm sure I've mentioned him before. I've been reading through his *Works* for several years now (there are twenty-four volumes, averaging about 600 pages each!), and when I was working through his treatment on apostasy in volume 7, I came across a short, but insightful, passage on the "proper end and design" of evangelical truths. I want to share it with you.

Owen is discussing the first of six causes of apostasy from the gospel, namely, "that rooted enmity which is in the minds of men unto spiritual things, abiding uncured under the profession of the gospel." Owen demonstrates that when the gospel doesn't fully penetrate a person's heart, so as to bring about the intended transformation of the heart in particular ways, then the hostility of the unregenerate nature eventually rises up against the truth, even if there has been an outward profession of faith. But in arguing for this point, Owen takes some time to articulate just what are the intended effects of the gospel—the "proper end and design" of evangelical truths. There are three of them, which I will state in my own words, followed by some excerpts from Owen.

Rest and satisfaction in Christ. The first goal of the gospel is to "take off the soul of man from rest and satisfaction in itself" and to "seek after righteousness, life, peace, and blessedness, by Jesus Christ." The natural inclination of fallen human beings is to look inward at ourselves and what we can accomplish. Our problems may be moral, psychological, or spiritual, but the core conviction of our untransformed hearts is this: "I can do it. I can handle this." So we try to live better lives, to be better people, and to find within ourselves the resources we need for goodness and happiness (or in Owen's words, "righteousness, life, peace, and blessedness").

But the gospel "presseth to take men off wholly from their old foundations." It shows us our insufficiency and redirects our trust to Christ and his sufficiency alone. The gospel shows us that "present peace" and "future blessedness" are found not in ourselves or in anything we can do but only in Jesus.

Renovation of the soul. The second goal of the gospel is the "the renovation of our minds, wills, and affections, into the image or likeness of God." We are "predestined to be conformed to the image of [Christ]," says Paul (Romans 8:29), and the primary means God uses to effect this transformation is the gospel, applied to our hearts by the Spirit (2 Corinthians 3:18).

But how does this actually happen in practice? Owen answers: "by presenting spiritual things unto us in that light and evidence, with that power and efficacy, as to transform us into their likeness." In other words, transformation happens when the truth of the gospel comes into our hearts with both clarity and efficacy, logic and fire, conviction and passion, word and Spirit, light and heat.

A heart for worship. Finally, Owen says that evangelical truth "engageth the whole soul, in all its powers and faculties, through the whole course of its activity . . . to live unto God in all holy obedience." Worshiping God is the only rational response to the lavish mercies of God (Romans 12:1). But when the gospel does its work in our hearts, worship is not simply our duty to God (although it is) but the natural reflex of our hearts in response to God's revelation of his grace and mercy through the cross and resurrection of Christ and the gift of his Spirit.

Satisfaction, renovation, worship—these are the intended effects of the gospel in our lives. Every time we encounter the drama of redemption in the pages of Scripture or hear the good news of Christ crucified and risen proclaimed or come to the Lord's Table to feed on the body and blood of our Lord, we should be moved to this: deeper rest in Christ, greater likeness to Christ, and more vibrant worship of Christ.

To make the application concrete, I must ask myself whether the gospel has produced these effects in my heart. Is my trust firmly fixed on Christ and his cross, or am I still looking inward for moral improvement and existential satisfaction? Am I being more and more transformed into the image of Christ? Do I look more like Jesus than I did a year ago? Do I delight to worship God? Do the lavish mercies of God beckon my heart to praise and enjoy him?

If and when I must answer "no," perhaps it's because the gospel hasn't penetrated deeply enough. Maybe deep inside my soul, there is still an "uncured enmity" or hostility to God and the gospel. We must be watchful. When this is the case, Owen warns, "spiritual truths are first neglected, then despised, and at last, on easy terms, parted withal." Religious people sometimes profess to believe without really believing. When they do, they first "stifle truth as to its operation" and eventually "reject it as to its profession." This is the natural course of apostasy from the gospel. What a frightful warning.

But the remedy isn't simply to work harder. Rather, we need to embrace the gospel more deeply, with an earnest desire for the Spirit to apply the truths of the gospel more deeply and powerfully to our hearts.

Annie Dillard writes about someone who shot an eagle out of the sky and "found the dry skull of a weasel fixed by its jaws to his throat. The supposition is that the eagle had pounced on the weasel and the weasel swiveled and bit as instinct taught him, tooth to neck, and nearly won." It's a grim, even gruesome image, but Dillard applies it wisely:

I think it would be well, and proper, and obedient, and pure, to grasp your one necessity and not let it go, to dangle from it limp wherever it takes you. Then even death, where you're going no matter how you live, cannot you part. Seize it and let it seize you up aloft even, till your eyes burn out and drop; let your musky flesh fall off in shreds, and let your very bones unhinge and scatter, loosened over fields, over fields and woods, lightly, thoughtlessly, from any height at all, from as high as eagles.

We need that kind of weasel-like tenacity in holding on to the gospel. It suggests another great active-verb phrase used in Scripture (with which I'll close this letter) . . .

Hold fast!
Brian

P.S. You didn't mention anything about your church in your last letter. How are things going?

Embracing Community

Dear Chris,

I've got to admit, your letter really surprised me. I was under the impression that you were getting more deeply rooted in New Hope Covenant Church. At least, the last report I heard from you was positive. I do understand and even empathize with your discouragement. But don't you think this "disillusionment with the church" could be a slight overreaction?

I can't help but wonder if these feelings reflect a serious (though common) misconception about the community of faith. I could be wrong, but it seems to me that your expectations are off. I don't want to say they are too high, for many of the things you long for are thoroughly biblical. You are *right* to hunger for "relationships that aren't superficial." And practicing the "one another" commands in Scripture is *of course* an "essential feature of body life."

But remember that the "one anothers" work both ways and include not only the positive commands to love, pray for, and serve one another, but also harder-to-obey commands like forgiving and bearing with one another. Remember Paul's words:

> Put on then, as God's chosen ones, holy and beloved, compassionate hearts, kindness, humility, meekness, and patience, bearing with one another and, if one has a complaint against another, forgiving each other; as the Lord has forgiven you, so you also must forgive. And above all these put on love, which binds everything together in perfect harmony. (Colossians 3:12–14)

This is a tall order, to be sure! It's just not fun or easy to be humble, meek, patient, forbearing, and forgiving. And may I gently remind you that you can't even begin to obey these commands until people in your community start disappointing you and sinning against you?

I'm reminded of something Bonhoeffer said in his little book *Life Together*: "The serious Christian, set down for the first time in a Christian community, is likely to bring with him a very definite idea of what Christian life together should be and to try to realize it. But God's grace speedily shatters such dreams." Could it be that God, in his grace and providence, wants to use these feelings of disconnection and loneliness as a spur to help you let go of your own ideas about community and instead embrace the actual community you're now in, with all their warts and imperfections?

I'm not saying that a Christian should never leave a church to look for another. There are (a few) occasions when that may be necessary. But Chris, you've not even been a member of this church for an entire year. And based on all of your comments about New Hope in your letters and on the phone, I would say that this is a church where you have been both spiritually fed and cared for. Your pastor is a faithful shepherd who preaches the word in a Christ-exalting way. The church is orthodox in theology, practices church discipline, engages in evangelism and missions, and seems to care about the poor.

Now, I realize that none of these things address the problem of feeling disconnected and lonely. And I do understand the discouragement that can come from a negative small group experience. But I really don't think leaving the church is the solution. Maybe you should talk to your small group leader. Perhaps it would help to take more initiative in pursuing friendships with other members outside of the formal group meetings. There are a hundred practical things you could and should try. But even in doing this, don't let your ideas of "what community should be" become more important than the actual brothers and sisters with whom you've already vowed to live in covenant. As Bonhoeffer went on to say,

> Every human wish dream that is injected into the Christian community is a hindrance to genuine community and must be banished if genuine community is to survive. He who loves his dream of a community more than the Christian community itself becomes a

destroyer of the latter, even though his personal intentions may be ever so honest and earnest and sacrificial.

This, I believe, is both wise and right.

Let me close with one more thought. Although I'm trying to steer you away from thinking in a consumerist fashion about church, I do think it is also in *your* best interests to stay with New Hope. Here's why. Your relationship to the local church is in some ways (though, of course, not all) like marriage. The commitment is serious, and it must have a "for better or for worse" kind of persistent love to keep it strong and make it last.

There are all kinds of theological and sociological reasons for why this view of marriage is best. But one reason is that those who don't commit to one person for life often find themselves starting all over again two or even three or four times. But all things being equal, they lose some of their emotional capital every time. Thus, they lose some of the richness and depth that otherwise would have been possible for them.

I know, I know: in a less than ideal world, marriage doesn't always work like this. And I tend to think (though this is controversial, and I am far from certain) that Scripture allows divorce in some situations, such as adultery or abandonment. But there's no doubt that most people give up on marriage way too soon. And for all kinds of reasons that are sinful, selfish, and often silly.

And this holds true with the church as well. If you leave New Hope over these kinds of issues, what will keep you from leaving the next church for different reasons? And if that continues, how will you ever build deeper relationships that last for not only months but years? And how will you develop the kind of character that makes you a good church member, who regularly practices patience, forbearance, forgiveness, and love?

This hasn't been the easiest letter to write, partly because it is something of a rebuke. I hope you know that my motive in writing is love for you and a genuine desire for your well-being, the good of the church, and the honor of Christ who is Lord and Husband and Head of the church. Having sensed your humility and knowing your teachable spirit, I'm confident you will receive this letter in love and pray through it. May the Lord of the church give you guidance by his word and Spirit.

Yours in Christ,
Brian

Assurance of Salvation

Dear Chris,

Thank you for such a gracious and humble response, brother. It sounds like the Holy Spirit pulled you off the church-bashing detour before my letter ever reached you. Of course, the Spirit is a better (a gentler.) counselor than I am!

I am sorry, though, that I didn't discern the hidden root of your complaints. As a pastor, I feel that I should pick up on these things more quickly. I'm a bit frustrated at myself for missing it, to be honest. But that just shows the slowness of my own growth, doesn't it?

Well, it seems that the Spirit, working through your own meditation and prayer, has led you to a clear diagnosis. And I do understand how your struggles with assurance have been aggravated by the feelings of isolation. I think your present course of action is right. And I feel sure that moving toward your pastor to ask for spiritual care will help you and also help him as he shepherds you. Please let me know how it goes.

Now to your question. Yes, I do think genuine and lasting assurance is possible, though I also think many true believers find it elusive. It's important to remember that there is a vital distinction between faith and the assurance of faith. As chapter 18 of the Westminster Confession of Faith says, "This infallible assurance does not so belong to the essence of faith, but that a true believer may wait long, and conflict with many difficulties, before he be partaker of it." I hope you'll take some encouragement from remembering that a great many saints, including Wesley and our old friend John Bunyan, struggled through long and bitter seasons of doubt.

Nevertheless, I don't think this needs to be the case. Remember that John wrote his first letter with the goal of promoting assurance: "I write these things to you who believe in the name of the Son of

God that you may *know* that you have eternal life" (1 John 5:13). And while his letter is multi-layered, addressing numerous issues both doctrinal and practical, at least one of his aims is to list out the evidences by which people may know that they are truly born of God.

So how do we get and maintain assurance? I've found it helpful to think of assurance as a stool with several legs. All of the legs are important and necessary. Lose any one of them and the stool topples. These legs are (1) faith in the gospel promises of salvation, (2) evidences of God's grace in the transformation of the heart and life, (3) the testimony of the Holy Spirit, and (4) the fruit of love in relationships with other believers.

The first three of these are clearly listed in chapter 18, article 2, of the Westminster Confession:

> This certainty is . . . an infallible assurance of faith founded upon the divine truth of the promises of salvation (Hebrews 6:17–18), the inward evidence of those graces unto which these promises are made (2 Peter 1:4–5, 10–11; 1 John 2:3; 3:14; 2 Corinthians 1:12), the testimony of the Spirit of adoption witnessing with our spirits that we are the children of God (Romans 8:15–16), which Spirit is the earnest of our inheritance, whereby we are sealed to the day of redemption (Ephesians 1:13–14; 4:30; 2 Corinthians 1:21–22).

I think that's one of the best summaries of the basis for assurance that I've read. By the way, the pastors and theologians (or "divines," as they were called back then) who wrote the Confession included the references. You should look them up.

Now a couple of comments on each "leg."

(1) It is crucial, Chris, to start with faith in the gospel promises of salvation like "The saying is trustworthy and deserving of full acceptance, that Christ Jesus came into the world to save sinners" (1 Timothy 1:15) and "I am the resurrection and the life. Whoever believes in me, though he die, yet shall he live, and everyone who lives and believes in me shall never die" (John 11:25–26) and "The Spirit and the Bride say, 'Come.' And let the one who hears say, 'Come.' And let the one who is thirsty come; let the one who desires take the water of life without price" (Revelation 22:17).

We must start here, looking away from ourselves to Christ offered to sinners in the gospel, lest we confuse Christ's righteousness (the basis of our salvation) with our own works (the fruit of salvation). Owen, in his great book on forgiveness, warned about mixing foundation work with building work. What he meant was that we shouldn't focus on our obedience when we should be focusing on the obedience of Christ in our place. Justification precedes sanctification.

(2) But Scripture does teach us to look for the evidences of grace and new birth. Check out 1 John 2:29, 3:9, 4:7, 5:1, 5:4, and 5:18. But remember that these evidences always flow from faith and are never perfect this side of glory. So don't look for perfection. But you should mortify sin, cultivate the fruit of the Spirit, and do all that you can to fertilize and water the seed of the word in your heart. "Kill your corruptions and grow your graces," I like to say. For more on this, see chapters 7 and 8 in my book *Christ Formed in You.*

(3) The witness of the Spirit includes both objective and subjective aspects. Objectively, the Spirit seals and secures us (Ephesians 1:13; 4:30), dwells in our hearts (Romans 8:9), leads us to put sin to death (Romans 8:12–14), and gradually transforms us, making us more like Christ as we behold his glory (2 Corinthians 3:18). He does this for all believers, whether they can always perceive his work or not.

Yet he also works subjectively such that we *experience* his power and presence in a way that leads us to assurance: "For you did not receive the spirit of slavery to fall back into fear, but you have received the Spirit of adoption as sons, by whom we cry, 'Abba! Father!' The Spirit himself bears witness with our spirit that we are children of God" (Romans 8:15–16). You should pray for this and patiently wait for God to answer.

(4) This one may be the most overlooked, but have you ever thought about John's words in 1 John 3:14? "We know that we have passed out of death into life, because we love the brothers. Whoever does not love abides in death." This, again, is one reason why I think your ongoing commitment to a local church is so important. Your growing love for others (not theirs for you, as important as that is) is actually one strand of evidence that your faith is real. Remember Paul's words: what matters is "faith working through love" (Galatians 5:6).

I realize that these thoughts on assurance are just cursory at best. I hesitated to even write when I thought about both how difficult this must be for you and how limited my involvement actually is. The best counsel I can give is to keep using all the means of grace, open your heart to your pastor, and, especially, keep your eyes on Jesus, the great friend of sinners. God is neither reluctant to save nor stingy with his gifts, Chris. He has already demonstrated the depth of his love in sending his Son to the cross. So I leave you with that greatest of all promises: "He who did not spare his own Son but gave him up for us all, how will he not also with him graciously give us all things?" (Romans 8:32).

Yours,
Brian

The Subtle Danger of Self-Trust

Dear Chris,

Okay, since you've really pressed me for more, I'll try to give my perspective. Now that we've been corresponding regularly for awhile and have punctuated these letters with a couple of phone calls, I do think I've detected a pattern in your letters that might be helpful in diagnosing some of your spiritual maladies. My instincts may be wrong, of course, so take this for what it's worth.

It seems that since our correspondence began, you have gone through several cycles of discouragement and spiritual dryness, followed by repentance and renewed spiritual discipline, followed by a short season of satisfying fellowship with God only to land soon in the desert of the soul once again. This season of desolation is usually short, and when you renew the disciplines, joy returns. The question is, what prompts this interruption of communion with God in the first place? What perpetuates this cycle?

The encouraging thing is that there doesn't appear to be any *obvious* sin leading to the downfall. You have, for the most part, kept the hounds of lust, greed, and anger at bay. The external structures in your life generally protect you from your own passions. I also don't think the problem is circumstantial. You have your own unique trials to face and burdens to bear, of course. But these circumstances are present in your ups and your downs. So I think the underlying issue is more subtle.

The problem, I think, is self-sufficiency, self-reliance, self-trust. This causes you sometimes to grow careless and at other times to become overly introspective. When you're introspective, you usually end up discouraged. When you're careless, spiritual drowsiness kicks in. And like Bunyan's pilgrim, you soon find yourself sleeping on the

Enchanted Ground. Spurgeon called it the "Arbor of Sloth." As you can see, we're back to the topic of acedia.

I don't have much more to say about acedia as such. But I wanted to offer a couple of thoughts about how to break this cycle—how to prevent the spiritual decline. Once again, I find help in the prophet Jeremiah. In chapter 17, the Lord uses two images of trees to contrast two kinds of people: the desert shrub pictures those who turn away from the Lord to trust people instead, while the tree planted by water portrays those who place their trust firmly in the Lord.

> Cursed is the man who trusts in man
>   and makes flesh his strength,
>   whose heart turns away from the Lord.
> He is like a shrub in the desert,
>   and shall not see any good come.
> He shall dwell in the parched places of the wilderness,
>   in an uninhabited salt land.
>
> Blessed is the man who trusts in the Lord,
>   whose trust is the Lord.
> He is like a tree planted by water,
>   that sends out its roots by the stream,
> and does not fear when heat comes,
>   for its leaves remain green,
> and is not anxious in the year of drought,
>   for it does not cease to bear fruit. (Jeremiah 17:5–8)

These two images show us the difference between the person who flourishes spiritually and the person who doesn't.

And note: the difference is not circumstantial. Both the shrub in the desert and the flourishing tree experience "heat." But the flourishing tree endures and remains fruitful through the year of drought. The difference is in their respective root systems—an apt metaphor for where we place our trust. While the first person trusts in man and makes flesh his strength, the flourishing person is Godward. He trusts in the Lord and is like a tree planted by water, thrusting his roots downward into the Lord himself, the fountain of living water (see Jeremiah 17:13 and compare 2:13). That's why he doesn't fear the heat, isn't anxious in the year of drought, and keeps on bearing fruit.

I want to be (and want you to be) that kind of person. I want to face the heat of suffering and the drought of affliction with the kind of resilient faith that will continue to bear fruit. But that kind of confidence doesn't come from our own hearts. As Jeremiah says in 17:9, "The heart is deceitful above all things, and desperately sick; who can understand it?" Confidence comes, then, only from the Lord himself.

The lesson to learn, dear brother, is this: don't trust in your emotions about God. Trust God. Your emotions are not a reliable indicator of God's presence or blessing in your life. Sometimes you will *feel* like he's not the stream of living water that he is. Witness Jeremiah's own disorientation in 17:14–18. Distrust those feelings and trust God anyway. In time you will find, as Jeremiah did, that God was sustaining you all along.

Remember the lines of that great hymn "Solid Rock"?

> My hope is built on nothing less
> Than Jesus' blood and righteousness;
> I dare not trust the sweetest frame,
> But wholly lean on Jesus' Name.
>
> When darkness seems to hide his face,
> I rest on his unchanging grace;
> In every high and stormy gale,
> My anchor holds within the veil.
>
> His oath, his covenant, his blood
> Support me in the whelming flood;
> When all around my soul gives way,
> He then is all my Hope and Stay.

In each of these stanzas, faith transcends feelings. The hymn writer acknowledges that God is greater than our circumstances or our feelings about them. Not just the negative emotions ("when darkness seems to hide his face") but even the positive ("I dare not trust the sweetest frame").

Perhaps I am wrong, but I think this is the heart of your problem: you rely too much on your emotions. You check your pulse too often. Your focus is too much on your self and not enough on Christ.

Let me draw this letter to a close with another word from John Owen. Near the end of his magnificent volume on *The Glory of Christ*, Owen writes about the causes and cure of "spiritual decay" and gives us the real key to preventing such backsliding and decline:

> Let us live in the constant contemplation of the glory of Christ, and virtue will proceed from him to repair all our decays, to renew a right spirit within us. . . . The most of our spiritual decays and barrenness arise from an inordinate admission of other things into our minds; for these are they that weaken grace in all its operations. But when the mind is filled with thoughts of Christ and his glory, when the soul thereon cleaves unto him with intense affections, they will cast out, or not give admittance unto, those causes of spiritual weakness and indisposition.

So do not be discouraged, even when you fail to trust him! To linger in discouragement is to persist in looking at yourself rather than at Christ. The truth is that no one has ever lived an uninterrupted life of full flourishing except Jesus himself. But the gospel reminds us that though he himself was like a tree rooted in the streams of his Father's love, he was treated like a shrub in the wilderness. For on the cross, he took our curse (Galatians 3:13). He withered in the heat of divine judgment so that we could flourish in the stream of God's love.

Sola Fide,
Brian

Developing a Spiritual Growth Plan

Dear Chris,

If you haven't totally sworn off New Year's resolutions yet, what are your goals for this year? What is your plan for spiritual growth? To *grow*, as you know, is another key scriptural metaphor for Christian spirituality—an organic metaphor picturing the process of maturation from infancy to adulthood or seed to fruit-bearing plant. Occasionally, we see the word *grow* used in an architectural context to describe the gradual construction of a building or edifice (hence, the Christian use of the word *edification*). When these images are applied to believers, whether as individuals or as communities, the implication is that maturity comes organically, gradually, incrementally.

But also deliberately. We are, after all, *commanded* to grow (see 2 Peter 3:18). Contrary to what some people may think or desire, spiritual transformation doesn't happen instantaneously or automatically. Rather, change is an intentional process. It requires planning.

So I want to challenge you to develop a plan for spiritual growth. There are many different models to follow. I was inspired years ago by Jonathan Edwards' Resolutions, many of them written when he was just nineteen years old. They continue to influence my thinking about spiritual development and change. He was a rare exemplar of self-discipline, time management, and personal holiness. He also framed his resolutions with a clear sense of his own inadequacies and dependence on God's grace.

Here is a matrix built around six aspects of life: knowledge, relationships, character, stewardship, service, and gospel.

1. First, *knowledge*. Christians today often pit knowledge against love, but Scripture keeps them together. Paul says that it's his prayer "that your love may abound more and more, with knowledge and

all discernment" (Philippians 1:9). Is your love for God and others an informed love, supported by and furnished with truth? And are you grounded in basic Christian theology? Or are there holes in your knowledge of Scripture? Defects in your worldview? Flaws in your theology? What will you do to grow in knowledge? One of my goals this year is to read through the Bible using M'Cheyne's reading plan.

2. Think next about your *relationships*. We are to abound not only in knowledge but in love. Are you reflecting the love of Christ to those closest to you? Are your friendships characterized by integrity, honesty, and faithfulness? Are you modeling godliness? To be more concrete, Chris, apply this to your local church situation. I gather that you're in a better place emotionally than you were a few weeks ago, but it would be easy to slip back into discouragement and even disillusionment. So it may be helpful to think about prayerfully pursuing two or three deeper relationships. George Sweeting, former chancellor of Moody, once said that everyone needs a Paul, a Barnabas, and a Timothy—that is, a mentor, a partner, and a disciple. Who fills these shoes in your life? Are there people in your small group or who live in your neighborhood that you should go after?

3. *Character*, of course, is not isolated from our relationships to others. But it is possible to be outwardly kind while our inward impulses lie elsewhere. We need to plow deeper, turning up the soil of the drives, motives, and desires of our hearts. And we need to look for patterns in our lives. There is a shape to your personhood. The question is how closely does it conform to the contours of Christ? Think of the fruit of the Spirit (Galatians 5) or Paul's description of love (1 Corinthians 13). Do these passages describe you? Are you generous, content, grateful, temperate, kind, and self-effacing? If someone were to play a video of your thought life, would you be ashamed and embarrassed? What needs to change in your self-talk?

4. Sometimes the best index of our character is in how we use our resources, so we must think about *stewardship*. How strategically do you invest your energy, time, and money? Where do you log the most hours and spend the most dollars? Think especially of discretionary time and money: do you use these resources for the common good, or do you squander them on self-centered pursuits? If others

examined your calendar and your credit card statement, what kind of person would they think you are?

5. The measure of our likeness to Christ is seen concretely in our *service* to others. Jesus climbed for the bottom, not the top (Philippians 2). He didn't hanker for position but abandoned privilege in order to serve God and man. How are you serving the church and the world? Are you a church consumer: attending, sitting, hearing, receiving, but not doing, serving, giving? What about your community? Is your "ministry" limited to those inside the church? Maybe you should volunteer to serve the homeless in a soup kitchen or visit the elderly in a nursing home or spend vacation time building a house with Habitat for Humanity.

6. The danger in everything I've written so far is to cause us to become overly introspective and self-reliant (something to which both of us are already prone!). Goals are good, but they are not *gospel*. Just as God's law is holy, just, and good, but also damning, so are some of our best intentions. More than anything else, we need to be grounded in the realities of the gospel: the good news of what God has done to rescue sinners and restore the world through the death, burial, and resurrection of Jesus. But the gospel doesn't absolve us from intentionality in transformation. Gospel is not anti-law. No, the truth of the gospel empowers obedience by transforming us deeply, giving us a new set of motivations, and reorienting us to God and grace. The formula is not more gospel and fewer goals, but more gospel with transformed goals and new power.

Finally, don't forget that growth takes time. Several months ago, my daughter Susannah decided she wanted to plant a cherry tree, and Holly told her she could plant it in our backyard. An hour or so later, Suz came in with a gloomy face, so Holly asked how the planting went. With a long, heavy sigh, our daughter replied, "It didn't grow!" Sometimes I think we're just as impatient with growth in our spiritual lives. Remember Newton's hymn "Prayer, Answered by Crosses."

Grace and peace,
Brian

Gospel Humility

Dear Chris,

I have often felt the same. But don't let this apparent lack of progress discourage you. I see increasing evidences of God's grace in your life, even if you do not. Sometimes I think God even keeps us from seeing our own growth in grace clearly in order to keep us dependent on him. Remember, growing spiritually doesn't mean getting more and more self-sufficient, but gaining more awareness of how absolutely dependent we are on him for everything! The branches derive all their life from the vine, and "apart from [Jesus] you can do nothing" (John 15:5).

What we need is gospel humility that is neither blind about nor despairing over our sin. John Bunyan is a good model. And no, this time I'm not going to quote *The Pilgrim's Progress*! Bunyan wrote *Grace Abounding to the Chief of Sinners* years after his conversion to tell the story of his spiritual journey. Near the end of that book, he wrote,

> I find to this day seven abominations in my heart: 1. Inclining to unbelief; 2. Suddenly to forget the love and mercy that Christ manifesteth; 3. A leaning to the works of the law; 4. Wanderings and coldness in prayer; 5. To forget to watch for that I pray for; 6. Apt to murmur because I have no more, and yet ready to abuse what I have; 7. I can do none of those things which God commands me, but my corruptions will thrust in themselves. When I would do good, evil is present with me.
>
> These things I continually see and feel, and am afflicted and oppressed with, yet the wisdom of God doth order them for my good; 1. They make me abhor myself; 2. They keep me from trusting my heart; 3. They convince me of the insufficiency of all inherent righteousness; 4. They show me the necessity of flying to Jesus; 5.

They press me to pray unto God; 6. They show me the need I have to watch and be sober; 7. And provoke me to pray unto God, through Christ, to help me, and carry me through this world.

There is a wealth of wisdom in Bunyan's self-reflection and confession, wisdom that most Christians (myself included) all too often lack. Before you write Bunyan off as overly introspective or as someone with excessively low self-esteem, consider this. Isn't it the case, more often than not, that we tend to be either (1) essentially blind to our own sins and apathetic in our love for Jesus, or (2) so devastated with our faults, sins, and inadequacies that we feel depressed, maybe even debilitated?

Bunyan provides a different model. He shows us what gospel humility really looks like—neither too blind to acknowledge sin, nor too despairing to feel hope and confidence and joy. Bunyan was relentlessly honest with himself about his sinful inclinations. He didn't trust his own heart. But at the same time, he let this honest self-assessment drive him to Jesus and to greater vigilance and prayer. Whatever you might think when you read words like "they make me abhor myself," Bunyan didn't wallow in despondent guilt. Rather, he let the sight of his sin drive him to the Savior. You and I should do the same.

Brian

P.S. After finishing this letter last night, I started thinking about your comment regarding sanctification being by faith alone. I think I agree, if you mean that faith must be the root of all our effort. Scripture backs that: without faith, we cannot please God (Hebrews 11:6), and "whatever does not proceed from faith is sin" (Romans 14:23), faith works through love (Galatians 5:6), and the life we live is by faith in the Son of God (Galatians 2:20). I could go on.

But it is easy to veer into unbiblical extremes. If you mean that sanctification requires no effort on our part, I disagree. If you mean that the classic spiritual disciplines of prayer, meditation, worship, and so on, are just exercises in legalism, I disagree. If you mean that all moral exhortation necessarily leads to moralism, I disagree. If you mean that no other motive (such as fear) can help us spiritually, I disagree (see 2 Corinthians 7:1; Philippians 2:12). Or if you mean that some special kind of faith ushers us into a higher, deeper, or more victorious life, I disagree.

J. C. Ryle warned against this last error in his classic book *Holiness*. He was countering the popular teaching of the nineteenth-century holiness conferences, which tended to pit faith against effort in unbiblical ways. It's the old "let go and let God" theology that decries the call to effort and the experience of struggle or conflict as acting in the "energy of the flesh" instead of the Spirit. I'm convinced that this is a false trail usually leading to confusion and disillusionment on the one hand and naïveté or even pride on the other.

I think the Belgic Confession gets the balance right (I've included Article 24 below for your reference). More could be said, but this postscript is getting too long!

Belgic Confession of Faith
Article 24: Of man's sanctification and good works

We believe that this true faith, produced in man by the hearing of God's Word and by the work of the Holy Spirit, regenerates him and makes him a "new man," causing him to live the "new life" and freeing him from the slavery of sin.

Therefore, far from making people cold toward living in a pious and holy way, this justifying faith, quite to the contrary, so works within them that apart from it they will never do a thing out of love for God but only out of love for themselves or fear of being condemned.

So then, it is impossible for this holy faith to be unfruitful in a human being, seeing that we do not speak of an empty faith but of what Scripture calls "faith working through love," which leads a man to do by himself the works that God has commanded in his Word.

These works, proceeding from the good root of faith, are good and acceptable to God, since they are all sanctified by his grace. Yet they do not count toward our justification—for by faith in Christ we are justified, even before we do good works. Otherwise they could not be good, any more than the fruit of a tree could be good if the tree is not good in the first place.

So then, we do good works, but not for merit—for what would we merit? Rather, we are indebted to God for the good works we do, and not he to us, since it is he who "works in us both to will and to do according to his good pleasure"—thus keeping in mind what is written: "When you have done all that is commanded you, then you shall say, 'We are worthy servants; we have done what it was our duty to do.'"

Yet we do not wish to deny that God rewards good works—but it is by his grace that he crowns his gifts.

Moreover, although we do good works we do not base our salvation on them; for we cannot do any work that is not defiled by our flesh and also worthy of punishment. And even if we could point to one, memory of a single sin is enough for God to reject that work.

So we would always be in doubt, tossed back and forth without any certainty, and our poor consciences would be tormented constantly if they did not rest on the merits of the suffering and death of our Savior.

Resting in Jesus

Dear Chris,

Let me back into a response by unearthing my own past. When I was twenty years old, I heard a message from an old preacher based on Matthew 11:28–30, which he called, "The Yoke: Are You in It?" This was almost nineteen years ago, so I'm sketchy on the details, but his basic thrust was that there are two "rests" in this passage: when we first come to Jesus for salvation, we get the first rest (verse 28), but only when we take the yoke of Christ through a crisis of deep, personal surrender do we get the second rest (the "rest for your souls" mentioned in verse 29).

It was a compelling talk, and it hit me at an important stage in my walk with Jesus. I was single and wrestling with God's will about a potential romantic relationship. I was struggling with sins of various sorts (especially lust!) and I desperately wanted to grow. This message promised something that I longed for: deep rest that comes from being yoked in the plow with Jesus Christ. I wanted to be free from struggle and conflict. I wanted this elusive, promising, mystical "rest"—whatever it was. So I prayed yet another prayer of surrender (it wasn't the first) in hopes of getting whatever I lacked.

But nothing really changed. Within a couple of weeks, I was faced with the same old struggles. I was confused and starting to grow cynical. When I heard a similar talk a few months later, I walked out of a crowded room during the invitation, thoroughly disillusioned with the whole idea of depending on crisis experiences for spiritual growth. I still wanted to follow Jesus, but this whole approach didn't seem to be working.

Over the next several years, I started reading guys like Michael Horton (*Putting Amazing Back into Grace*), J. I. Packer (*Keep in Step with the Spirit*), and J. C. Ryle (*Holiness*), and I came to understand what had happened: I had swallowed a version of second-blessing, two-stage sanctification, deeper-life theology hook, line, and sinker. Over time, I came to see that struggle was normal—not necessarily an indication that I still lived in the "energy of the flesh." I realized that I was engaged in a lifelong fight against sin, but I also saw that thoroughgoing faith in Christ's finished work could give me true rest, regardless of my daily performance with all the victories and defeats. Here was a theology of sanctification (and justification!) that made good sense of Scripture and mapped onto my experience in a much more convincing way. I have happily inhabited the Augustinian-Reformed doctrine of sanctification ever since.

I've tipped my hand in past letters, so I'm sure my position is no surprise to you. But now you may understand why. I am suspicious of the "second blessing" approaches to holiness because they promise a kind of rest that seems out of sync with the whole of Scripture. As much as I love the Wesleys, I think they (and their theological descendants) got it wrong here. I discuss the problems with "deeper life" teaching in a bit more detail in one of my books, but if you really want to dig deep, go to chapters 3 and 4 of Packer's *Keep in Step with the Spirit*.

With all of that personal background and theological context, I still haven't answered your question! So what about resting in Jesus? Didn't Augustine himself teach that God has made us for himself such that our hearts are restless until they rest in him? Or consider that old hymn from Proctor and Sankey:

> Cast your deadly "doing" down—
> Down at Jesus' feet;
> Stand in Him, in Him alone,
> Gloriously complete.

Isn't there something profoundly *right* about this? If so, where does all my talk about effort fit in? These are good and important questions, so let me attempt an answer in two parts.

1. First, when Jesus invites us to take his yoke and enter his rest, he is calling us to trust in him for salvation. Whom does he invite?

The weary and burdened. He calls those who are weary with sin and burdened with guilt—those living under the "yoke" of the law.

Biblical scholars tell us that "yoke" was a familiar image in ancient agrarian cultures and that it was often used metaphorically, sometimes to refer to slavery or servitude. That is why Paul addressed slaves in 1 Timothy 6:1 as "all who are under a yoke as bondservants." Sometimes the word *yoke* would carry the idea of judgment. For example, the Old Testament warned the Israelites that if they would not serve the Lord with joyfulness and gladness of heart, then they would serve their enemies; the Lord would put a yoke of iron on their necks until he destroyed them (Deuteronomy 28:47–48). In other words, slavery to enemies would be a form of God's judgment.

At other times, the word *yoke* carried the connotation of a student's submission to his teacher. When the rabbis invited people to become students or disciples of the law and traditions, they actually called it taking the yoke of the law. Ben Sirach, in the Apocryphal book of Ecclesiasticus, actually said, "Put your neck under the yoke, and let your soul receive instruction" (Ecclesiasticus 51:26). This is also reflected in the words of Peter recorded in Acts 15:10 to the Jerusalem council when they were trying to determine whether Jesus-following Gentiles should be circumcised or not. Peter said, "Why are you putting God to the test by placing a yoke on the neck of the disciples that neither our fathers nor we have been able to bear?"

So when Jesus calls out to the weary and burdened and invites them to come to him for rest, and then to take his yoke, those who heard him knew exactly what he meant. He meant "Quit following the teaching of the rabbis. Give up this endless list of rules. Stop being disciples of Torah as interpreted by the rabbis. Instead, come to me and be my disciples, my students. Take my yoke instead of theirs." It was a radical call to trust in Jesus rather than Torah to save them. Jesus was essentially teaching justification by faith.

2. The second thing to say is this: whatever rest Jesus promises here, it doesn't mean the absence of all conflict, struggle, work, or striving. In fact, Jesus himself tells us to strive (Luke 13:24). Resting in Jesus for salvation doesn't mean the absence of all striving but the presence of a certain kind of striving. We're not to trust in ourselves—

our own strength, obedience, righteousness, merit, or works—but in him.

Trusting in him isn't always easy, of course. Sometimes it involves a fight.

One of the best explanations of this tension that I've read is from John Piper's book *Future Grace*. It's a few paragraphs long, but well worth reading. Having raised this tension between striving and resting, Piper writes this:

Can [the life of faith] be both hard and easy?

Yes. Faith in future grace is intrinsically easy. What could be easier than trusting God to work for you (Isaiah 64:4), and take care of you (1 Peter 5:7), and give you all you need (Philippians 4:19; Hebrews 13:6), and strengthen you for every challenge (Isaiah 41:10). In one sense, faith is the opposite of straining. It is ceasing from the effort to earn God's approval or demonstrate your worth or merit. It is resting in the gracious promises of God to pursue us with goodness and mercy all our days. Faith is intrinsically easy.

But this ease of faith assumes that our hearts are humble enough to renounce all self-reliance and self-direction and self-exaltation. It assumes a heart that is spiritual enough to taste and delight in the beauty and worth of God. It assumes that the world and the devil have lost their power to lure us away from satisfaction in God. If these assumptions are not true, then living by faith in future grace will not be as easy as we might have thought, but will involve a lifetime of struggle.

It's like the monkey with his hand caught in the jar. It would be easy for him to slip his hand out of the opening except that he has his fist clenched around the nut. If he loves the nut more than he loves freedom from the jar, then getting his hand out of the jar will be hard, even impossible . . . But what could be easier than dropping a nut? The battle that Paul and Jesus are talking about is the battle to love the freedom of faith more than the nut of sin.

So the first thing we can say about a lifetime of keeping the faith is that it is like a race and a fight. It involves relentless warfare and vigilance.

That was really helpful for me when I first read it, and it has lingered in my mind ever since. Whenever I try to make sense of the tension between effort and faith, between struggle and rest, I remember, "The struggle is as easy as dropping a nut."

Well, as is usually the case when I sit down to write these letters, I have an abundance of words and a shortage of time. So I must stop. I hope this has helped a little, and I look forward to further discussion.

In Christ,
Brian

The Race Set Before Us

Dear Chris,

It's hard to believe that spring is almost here! Between my normal work schedule and the frantic pace of life with four kids, I'm afraid I've fallen out of my routine and failed to respond to your last several letters. Please don't interpret my silence as lack of love or concern for you. I'm always happy to get your letters and am glad I finally have time to sit down and put some thought into a reply.

Regarding your growing joy in worship, it's no accident that this has coincided with your deepening theological study. More often than not, the heart follows the head. Spurgeon once said, "The coals of orthodoxy are necessary to the fires of piety," and C. S. Lewis confessed that he found "the doctrinal books more helpful in devotion than the devotional books," thinking that others "would find that the heart sings unbidden while they are working their way through a tough bit of theology with a pipe in their teeth and a pencil in their hand."

Knowing your penchant for pipes, I thought you'd appreciate that.

I've been thinking again about the athletic metaphors for the Christian life. Ever since we started writing, I've intended to write something about the race metaphor. And, of course, I've recommended the Schreiner and Caneday book (have you read it yet?) that was so formative in my thinking several years ago.

Running the race may be Paul's most vivid metaphor for the active nature of the Christian life. He uses it, for example, in 1 Corinthians 9:

> Do you not know that in a race all the runners compete, but only one receives the prize? So run that you may obtain it. Every athlete exercises self-control in all things. They do it to receive a perishable wreath, but we an imperishable. So I do not run aimlessly; I do not

box as one beating the air. But I discipline my body and keep it under control, lest after preaching to others I myself should be disqualified. (1 Corinthians 9:24-27)

It's helpful to get a mental picture of what Paul has in mind. He was writing to the believers in Corinth, an ancient city just fourteen kilometers away from an athletic arena in Isthmia. Scholars tell us that games were held in Isthmia every two years, attracting thousands of people from all over the Roman Empire. Paul himself was probably in Corinth during the Games of A.D. 51, so both he and his friends in Corinth knew the games well.

First, think about the race itself. The arena for the games was known as the *agon* (the root of our words *agony* or *agonize*). The *agon* was the stadium where the contests were held and could refer to the competition itself; in time, *agon* referred to any kind of conflict (not only in athletics). Paul uses a cognate of this word when he says "every athlete exercises self-control" (*agonizomai*). This word is used six times in the New Testament: half apply metaphorically to the Christian life of faith (1 Timothy 6:12; 2 Timothy 4:7; Hebrews 12:1) while the other three refer to conflicts endured for the gospel (Philippians 1:30; Colossians 2:1; 1 Thessalonians 2:2).

It's not difficult to see the application of the metaphor. The Christian life is a race that requires both determined effort and dogged perseverance. Of course, Scripture also uses the metaphor of *rest* to describe the life of faith (Matthew 11:28-30), but the Christian life isn't only rest—it's also an endurance test. To quote Isaac Watts, we don't make our journey on "flow'ry beds of ease, while others fight to win the prize and sail through bloody seas." Our old friend, John Bunyan, in a short book about 1 Corinthians 9:24 called *The Heavenly Footman*, saw three things implied in the race: "flying . . . pressing . . . continuing." He also envisioned the race as something of an obstacle course: "The way is long, and there is many a dirty step, many a high hill, much work to do, a wicked heart, the world, and devil to overcome."

But it's not enough to know about the race. We must also think about the *crown*, the *prize* for which we run. The competitors in the Isthmian Games ran for a wreath made of celery or pine—thus a *perishable* crown. But Paul says that we run for a crown that's imperishable. The word *crown* pops up eighteen times in the New Testament, with at least five of those referring to a crown that will be received on the last day. For example, there is the crown of righteousness (2 Timothy 4:8), the crown of life (James 1:12; Revelation 2:10), the crown of glory (1 Peter 5:4), the crown of honor (Philippians 4:1; 1 Thessalonians 2:19), and the imperishable crown (1 Corinthians 9:25). Just what is this crown? While some interpreters have viewed the crown as some kind of heavenly reward for the faithful, it seems more in keeping with the tone of Paul and the other writers to see the crown as a metaphor for eternal life itself.

Consider how John contrasts "crown of life" with the "second death" in Revelation 2:10–11. Also note the similar language with which Paul exhorts Timothy: "Fight the good fight of the faith. Take hold of the eternal life to which you were called and about which you made the good confession in the presence of many witnesses" (1 Timothy 6:12). In fact, the New Testament frequently uses the words *life*, *righteousness*, and *glory* to signify our future and final inheritance as believers. When the word *crown* is added, we know that these blessings are prizes worth running for. To quote Bunyan again, "They that will have heaven must run for it."

So running for the prize demands all-out effort on our part, but we mustn't think that the effort it demands is works-based law keeping. Paul clearly distances himself from this in Philippians 3, the other key passage on the race. Paul runs for the prize of "the surpassing worth of knowing Christ" (verse 8) for whose sake he counts all things, including his own righteousness, as rubbish. He is confident of being justified through "faith in Christ—the righteousness from God that depends on faith" (verse 9). But this doesn't make Paul apathetic. On the contrary, it unleashes in him the singular ambition of knowing Christ in both the power of his resurrection and the suffering of his death (verse 10). With his eyes on future resurrection (verse 11), Paul forgets what is behind and strains forward with every muscle and nerve in his being towards the finish line, pressing for the goal, eager to gain the prize to which God has called him in Christ (verses

12–14). Paul's words show us that the race of faith is nothing less than the active pursuit of God's glory, grounded in God's effective call of believers to himself.

Isaac Watts, once again, got it right. Here is his rousing call to run the race in the strength that God supplies:

> Awake, our souls; away, our fears
> Let every trembling thought begone;
> Awake, and run the heav'nly race,
> And put a cheerful courage on.
>
> True, 'tis a strait and thorny road,
> And mortal spirits tire and faint,
> But they forget the mighty God,
> That feeds the strength of every saint.

The race is often difficult and demands "our utmost for his highest." We need courage, to be sure. But we will not tire or faint as long as we remember "the mighty God that feeds the strength of every saint." While the stakes in this race are high, our final triumph is not in doubt, for Christ has already made us his own (Philippians 3:12). We run *for* glory, yes. But we run *because of* grace. And that makes all the difference.

Brian

Looking to Jesus

Dear Chris,

I'm really grateful for how the Lord is now using the church in your spiritual growth. Few things are more fortifying to our faith than consistent, heart-searching, Spirit-anointed, Christ-centered exposition of God's word. It sounds like you are being fed well and are settling nicely into your new small group.

Don't underestimate, however, the importance of the Lord's Table. Scripture doesn't prescribe how frequently we should celebrate it— only that "as often as" we eat the bread and drink the cup, we do so in remembrance of Christ. Since I was raised in a tradition that observed the Table less frequently, I can understand your initial hesitancy about weekly Communion. But I think you will find, as I have, that the more often you come to the Table, the more deeply you are helped.

Nor do I think your consciousness of indwelling sin and ongoing struggle should keep you from Communion. Yes, Paul warns the Corinthians not to eat or drink in an unworthy manner (1 Corinthians 11:27), but he is speaking specifically about the divisive practices of people in the Corinthian church. The rich were neglecting the poor and abusing the Table, getting drunk while others went hungry. The inherent divisiveness of their behavior was a practical denial of the very unity the Table is meant to portray (see 1 Corinthians 10:16–17 and 11:17–34, and consult Gordon Fee's particularly helpful commentary if you want more on the original context).

Of course, the general principle still applies. We should use the Table as an opportunity for self-examination and repentance. But also for renewed faith. No one has helped me deal with my own scrupulous conscience in this area more than Calvin:

When we feel within us a strong distaste and hatred of all vices, proceeding from the fear of God, and a desire to live well in order to please our Lord, we are fit to partake of the Supper, notwithstanding the vestiges of infirmity which we carry in our flesh.

He then compared the Table to medicine that Christ gives to heal our wounded hearts:

Since then it is a remedy which God has given us to assist our frailty, to fortify our faith, to augment our charity, and to further us in all sanctity of life, so far from this making us abstain, we ought the more to make use of it, the more we feel oppressed by the disease.

To refuse the Table because "we are still weak in faith or in integrity of life" would be like a person refusing to take medicine because he is sick. "This then," says Calvin, "is how the frailty of the faith which we feel in our heart, and the imperfections which persist in our life, ought to incite us to come to the Supper, as to a remedy designed to correct them. Only let us not come without faith or repentance." In other words, we must always come to the Table with eyes fixed on Jesus.

Which brings me back to your question about how we should run the race. Paul, along with the writer of Hebrews, suggests several features of an athlete's mentality. First of all, we need *intentionality*. We must run with the purpose of winning (see 1 Corinthians 9:24). Paul himself is an example for us: "I do not run aimlessly; I do not box as one beating the air" (1 Corinthians 9:26).

But this entails a second quality: *struggle*. "Every athlete exercises self-control in all things. They do it to receive a perishable wreath, but we an imperishable" (v. 25). Again, the word is *agonizomai*, from which we get our word *agonize*. Elsewhere, it is translated as *strive* ("strive to enter the narrow door" in Luke 13:34), *struggle* ("For this I toil, struggling with all his energy" in Colossians 1:29), or *fight* ("Fight the good fight of faith" in 1 Timothy 6:12).

We also need *discipline*. Scholars tell us that athletes could only compete in the Games after ten months of strict training, and Paul uses similarly pugilistic terms to describe his own self-mastery: "But

I discipline my body and keep it under control, lest after preaching to others I myself should be disqualified" (1 Corinthians 9:27). Or in William Barclay's terms, "I batter my body; I make it my slave." The more famous race passage in Hebrews 12 fills out the picture, for an athletic mentality specifically involves ridding our lives of things that hinder us from running well. We must "lay aside every weight, and sin which clings so closely" (verse 1). First-century athletes ran in the nude, so that clothing wouldn't entangle their feet, and Christians must metaphorically strip from our lives anything that keeps us from Jesus.

Next, we must "run with *endurance*" (Hebrews 12:1), for we're not only hindered by sin and distractions but by discouragement. Sometimes we just get weary. The older I get, the more I see the relevance of this passage for myself. I used to think of running the race with a bit too much triumphalism. I was like Eric Liddell—ready to take on any opposition no matter the cost. Now, I more often feel like Rocky Balboa in the fifteenth round with Apollo Creed. Life has beaten me black and blue, but I'm still standing, enduring, holding on for the sound of the bell.

So what can sustain us in this brutal contest of faith? See the next verse in Hebrews 12: "Looking to Jesus, the founder and perfecter of our faith, who for the joy that was set before him endured the cross, despising the shame, and is seated at the right hand of the throne of God." Here, then, is the fifth and most essential quality we need if we will run to win: *eyes fixed on Jesus*. No runner can get far down the track while watching his feet. He must set his eyes on the tape. And more than anything else, we must set our focus on Christ himself. Ultimately, he is the prize we're reaching for.

Looking to him,
Brian

Vincit Qui Patitur

Dear Chris,

Nope, I don't have any tattoos, though I don't object to them. But I'm old enough that if I got one, everyone would just think I was trying to be cool. They would probably be right. So I guess I'll remain uncool and untatted. At least for now!

If I *were* to get a tattoo, however, I'd be tempted to copy one of my friends who has the Latin phrase *Vincit qui patitur* ("He who suffers conquers") inscribed on his left forearm. It's from John Geree, a Puritan pastor who was ejected from his pulpit in 1646 and wrote *The Character of an Old English Puritan*. According to J. I. Packer, this phrase "was in practice the Puritan's motto."

That leads me to yet another one of the active metaphors from the New Testament: *conquer.* The Greek word is *nikao*, the verb form of the word *nike*. We know Nike as a brand of tennis shoes, but to the Greeks, Nike was the winged goddess of victory, the goddess who drove the chariot of Zeus and presided over the athletic games. Over and again, the authors of the New Testament (especially John) write of Christians conquering or overcoming. This vivid language shows us the need to fight for victory.

This language is especially prominent in the book of Revelation. Each of the seven letters in chapters 2 and 3 end with a promise "to the one who conquers" (2:7, 11, 17, 26–28; 3:5, 12, 21). As J. C. Ryle observed, "There are no promises in the Lord Jesus Christ's epistles to the seven churches, except to those who 'overcome.' Where there is grace there will be conflict. The believer is a soldier. There is no holiness without a warfare. Saved souls will always be found to have fought a fight."

As believers still waiting for glorification, we all have things we need to conquer. We all face obstacles to overcome. Some of these obstacles are *internal*, residing in our own hearts. Near the end of Revelation, there's a promise "to the one who conquers" that stands in contrast to those whose lives were dominated by sins of various kinds (21:6–9). The clear implication is that some have not conquered or overcome but have instead been conquered—by their own sins.

Of course, there are *external* obstacles as well. Particularly, "the world"—the wicked system of this present age which conspires against both God and goodness, appealing not to virtue, but vice, and aligning itself with the evil spiritual powers. Think of advertising that appeals to lust, economics that are driven by greed, or academic and athletic achievements that are motivated by pride. This is the world. But behind it all lurks the ancient serpent, Satan himself, the great Dragon (Revelation 12), the evil personality who rules as "the god of this world" (2 Corinthians 4:4).

The Scripture's analysis of our need is really profound. It acknowledges the things we feel to be our problems: greed, poverty, war, racism, imperialism, exploitation, abuse of power, personal suffering, and so on. But it does more. It probes further and digs deeper. It says that this darkness pervades not just the world but our own hearts, and it claims that the source of this darkness is an evil, malicious, spiritual power named Satan. But it also says that no one overcomes this darkness without a battle! You must take sides.

Yet the decisive triumph has already been won because "the Lion of the tribe of Judah, the Root of David, has conquered" (Revelation 5:5). This comes from John's vision of the throne room in chapters 4 and 5. And what's most remarkable about this vision is that when John looks for the Lion on the throne, what he sees is not a Lion but a Lamb: "And between the throne and the four living creatures and among the elders I saw a Lamb standing, as though it had been slain" (Revelation 5:6a).

This isn't as surprising for Christians today as it was for John, because we're used to thinking of Jesus as the Lamb who was slain. We sing songs about this now. But it wasn't so then—not yet. John would have thought of this as a surprising twist because he was learning that the conquering lion, the root of David, the Messiah of Israel and King of the world is a king who delivers his people through suffering. The lion is the lamb who was slain. Our king has conquered, but he has conquered through suffering and death—through the cross. That's how we conquer as well: "And they have conquered him by the blood of the Lamb and by the word of their testimony, for they loved not their lives even unto death" (Revelation 12:11).

How do we work this out practically? How do we conquer and overcome Satan, sin, and the world? John's answer (from his first letter) is new birth and faith: "For everyone who has been born of God overcomes the world. And this is the victory that has overcome the world—our faith. Who is it that overcomes the world except the one who believes that Jesus is the Son of God?" (1 John 5:4–5).

But what does overcoming faith look like?

Once again, I find Bunyan's *Pilgrim's Progress* a helpful guide. (As you see, I just can't get away from this book!) Think through the many obstacles Christian had to overcome. The Apollyon in the Valley of Humiliation, whom he conquered with the Armor of God and the Sword of the Spirit. And the Valley of the Shadow of Death, which Christian traversed with the help of All-Prayer. Then there was Vanity Fair, Bunyan's picture of the world with its varied temptations and snares. And so many more. Yet Christian perseveres through them all, eventually crossing the River of Death and inheriting eternal glory in the Celestial City.

From Bunyan's perspective as he wrote the story, Christian's final salvation was known and guaranteed from the beginning. Yet within the narrative itself, Christian had to fight and triumph through every trial and obstacle he faced on his journey. So it is with us. God knows and always has known who is called, chosen, and faithful. But we must still fight and triumph!

After Christian climbs the Hill of Difficulty, he has a short season of rest at the Palace Beautiful, but before he can enter the Palace he must pass two ferocious lions that guard the entrance. Christian feared that these lions would tear him to pieces, but he didn't see that they were chained. When Christian considers going back, the Porter of the Lodge named Watchful says to Christian, "Is thy Strength so small? Fear not the Lions, for they are chained, and placed there for the Trial of Faith, where it is, and for the Discovery of those who have none: keep in the midst of the Path, and no hurt shall come unto thee." So Christian stays on the path and, trembling with fear, passes between the lions. Bunyan wrote, "He heard them roar, but they did him no harm."

Once Christian has found safe lodging in Palace Beautiful, the lodge built by the Lord of the Hill "for the relief and security of Pilgrims," Christian talks to several young women named Prudence, Piety, and Charity. Prudence asks Christian what strategies he uses to vanquish, or conquer, the old sins that still annoy him. And Christian answers:

> When I think what I saw at the Cross, that will do it; and when I look upon my 'broidered Coat, that will do it; also when I look into the Roll that I carry in my bosom, that will do it, and when my thoughts wax warm about wither I am going, that will do it.

Bunyan's instruction is masterful. He is telling us that the way to overcome sin in our lives is to look to the cross, remember that we're covered in the righteousness of Christ (his embroidered Robe), remember that we are secure in our salvation (the Roll he carried in his bosom), and remember our final destiny, or let our thoughts "wax warm" about where we are going. This is how faith overcomes the world.

Vincit qui patitur!
Brian

The Preservation of the Saints

Dear Chris,

It was great to hear from you again this week. And praise God for his faithfulness, brother. Thanks for telling me about what you've been learning through church and in your devotional life. What thrills me most is how outward focused it all sounds. Rather than taking your own pulse, you seem taken up with the excitement of what you're learning about Jesus. And this, in turn, seems to be propelling you toward other people, both inside and outside the church. All of this seems very healthy to me. And you certainly don't need to apologize for writing less frequently. The help I could give you from this distance was seasonal at best. You're now receiving excellent pastoral care from your church, and I couldn't be happier.

I've being thinking about our correspondence over these past months. Though we've had occasion to discuss many things in our letters, the majority of mine to you have focused in one way or another on themes related to the classic Reformed doctrine of the perseverance of the saints. The active metaphors in Scripture point us in this direction again and again. I hope thinking through these has spurred your efforts in following the Lord and has also deepened your confidence in Christ himself. Of course, my part has been small. Your reading has been a huge part of this process. (I'm glad to hear you've finished Bunyan and Ryle and are finally working your way through Schreiner and Caneday.) But the Lord has especially used the church to meet these needs. This really is an answered prayer.

Anyway, given the overall "theme" of our correspondence, I thought it might be helpful to write one more letter about perseverance, but from a slightly different angle. You probably know that Reformed theologians write about both the *perseverance* and the *preservation* of the saints. They're really talking about the same doctrine, but from two different perspectives. If perseverance has to do with *our* responsibility to continue in faith and holiness, preservation highlights *God's* work in strengthening and sustaining our faith.

So much can be said about this side of the doctrine. John Owen wrote over 600 pages of careful theological argument, appealing to the immutability (unchangeableness) of God's nature and purpose, the covenant of grace and promises of God, the indwelling of the Holy Spirit, and the mediation and intercession of Christ, in his treatment of perseverance. But the Westminster Larger Catechism beautifully (and briefly!) summarizes the doctrine in question 79:

> May not true believers, by reason of their imperfections, and the many temptations and sins they are overtaken with, fall away from the state of grace?

> True believers, by reason of the unchangeable love of God, and his decree and covenant to give them perseverance, their inseparable union with Christ, his continual intercession for them, and the Spirit and seed of God abiding in them, can neither totally nor finally fall away from the state of grace, but are kept by the power of God through faith unto salvation.

Between Owen and the Westminster Larger Catechism, I see at least six or seven reasons why God preserves his saints and keeps them from falling away. And while I'm tempted to cram a mini-sermon into this letter and write about each of these, maybe it would serve you better if I highlighted just one. The one that probably nourishes and helps me the most is Christ's intercession. Let this truth sink deep into your heart, Chris: *Jesus prays for you.*

John 17 gives us a glimpse of Jesus praying for the church. And what does he pray? He prays that the Father will keep us in his name (verse 11), not taking us out of the world, but keeping us from the evil one (verse 15). He prays that we would be sanctified in the truth (verse 17), that we would be united (verses 20–21), and that we would come to see Christ's own glory, which the Father gave him before the foundation of the world (verse 24). It's a profound prayer that we sometimes call the "high priestly" prayer of Jesus.

And this is right, because Hebrews 7 shows us that Jesus, as our High Priest, continues to intercede for his people. Owen and other theologians have traditionally divided the priestly work of Christ into two aspects: his sacrifice and his intercession. Hebrews 7 shows us how these two things are distinct, yet related. In his sacrifice, Christ our High Priest offered himself for us once and for all (Hebrews 7:27). This is his finished and completed work. But now, he continues to apply this work to us through his ongoing intercessory prayer. And this guarantees complete salvation! "[Christ] holds his priesthood permanently, because he continues forever. Consequently, he is able to save to the uttermost those who draw near to God through him, since he always lives to make intercession for them" (Hebrews 7:24–25).

The story of Peter gives us a more personal understanding of Christ's intercession. Remember how Peter had brashly sworn his allegiance to Jesus, confident that he would never deny him? And Jesus warned him, "Simon, Simon, behold, Satan demanded to have you, that he might sift you like wheat" (Luke 22:31). Temptation is coming. Peter's faith will be tested. Indeed, he will stumble. But he will not be destroyed. Why? Because, says Jesus, "I have prayed for you that your faith may not fail" (verse 32).

And then there's Romans 8, maybe my favorite chapter in all of Scripture, where Paul asks, "Who is to condemn?" and triumphantly answers, "Christ Jesus is the one who died—more than that, who was raised—who is at the right hand of God, who indeed is interceding for us" (Romans 8:34).

Perhaps no one has captured the assurance borne of this doctrine better than Charitie Bancroft in his great hymn, "Before the Throne of God Above."

> Before the throne of God above
> I have a strong and perfect plea.
> A great high Priest whose Name is Love
> Who ever lives and pleads for me.
> My name is graven on His hands,
> My name is written on His heart.
> I know that while in Heaven He stands
> No tongue can bid me thence depart.

When Satan tempts me to despair
And tells me of the guilt within,
Upward I look and see Him there
Who made an end of all my sin.
Because the sinless Savior died
My sinful soul is counted free.
For God the just is satisfied
To look on Him and pardon me.

Behold Him there the risen Lamb,
My perfect spotless righteousness,
The great unchangeable I AM,
The King of glory and of grace,
One in Himself I cannot die.
My soul is purchased by His blood,
My life is hid with Christ on high,
With Christ my Savior and my God!

I couldn't find a better way to end this letter if I tried! So, I commend you, my friend, into the care and keeping of our faithful God. The Father has set his gracious eyes on you and loves you with an everlasting love. And he has sent his Son Jesus, our great High Priest, to live and die on your behalf. He has offered himself for your sins once and for all, and he now pleads his obedience and righteousness before the Father's gracious throne on your behalf. From that throne, the Father and Son have sent the Spirit into your heart, by which you now cry "Abba Father." The three-fold cord of our triune God's covenant grace cannot be broken. You are in good hands! Do stay in touch as you are able.

Yours in Christ,
Brian

Acknowledgements

So this is the page where I get to say thank you to the many people who helped this book make the journey from my brain space to your shelf space. And like all journeys through space, launching and landing this project required a team.

If I was the pilot, then Shepherd Press was Mission Control. I'm grateful not only for their interest in publishing *Active Spirituality* but for their willingness to chart a different course than any of us had in mind with the initial proposal.

A special thanks to Richard Riggall who, in addition to his many other responsibilities with Shepherd Press, served as navigational partner in the early stages of writing. Jennifer Strange kept me in orbit with her editing proficiency. Rick Irvin oversaw landing the craft, guiding the book through all the stages of production.

I'm also grateful to Anna Hedges, Andy Hedges, Terry Delaney, Tammi Mossman and especially Mark Schuitema, for serving as my pit crew by reading the first draft and offering helpful suggestions.

My beautiful wife Holly is also my best friend, copilot in life, and most insightful critic. She has always had a better sense of direction than me (in more ways than one!). Her honest critique of the first draft caused me to reroute and consequently arrive at a happier destination. Our four kids, Stephen, Matthew, Susannah, and Abby Taylor, fill our lives with joy and laughter. I love you all.

Finally, I'd like to dedicate this book to my grandparents, Arthur and Mozelle Hedges (a.k.a. Zanzan and Nanah), who blazed the trail before me. They have run the race and fought the good fight of faith. Their lives consistently display the Christian virtues of faith, hope, and love. I want to be like them when I grow up.

Notes on Sources

Full bibliographical details on books and articles mentioned in these notes and otherwise referenced in the letters can be found in the bibliography.

Opening Letter. "Not the labor of my hands" is the second verse of Augustus Toplady's hymn "Rock of Ages," composed in 1762.

The Pilgrim's Regress was the first book C. S. Lewis wrote as a Christian, and is both one of his most brilliant and one of his most difficult books. For Lewis, the North and South represented the philosophical dangers of overemphasizing objectivity and the intellect on one hand and sentimentality and the emotions on the other. I've obviously adapted the imagery for theological purposes.

Dietrich Bonhoeffer's famous passage about cheap grace is found in chapter 1 of *The Cost of Discipleship.*

In discussing the doctrine of perseverance, I'm quoting from chapter 17 of The Baptist Confession of 1689, which adapts and expands the same chapter from the Westminster Confession of Faith.

The quotation from Oswald Chambers is from the July 7 entry in *My Utmost for His Highest.*

Much of Luther's pastoral correspondence was published as *Letters of Spiritual Counsel* in *The Library of Christian Classics,* volume 18.

In crediting Lewis with baptizing my imagination, I'm echoing his own tribute to George MacDonald from chapter 11 of *Surprised by Joy.*

The final quotation is from Henriette Auber's 1829 hymn "Our blest Redeemer, 'ere he breathed."

Letter 1: Walking in the Way. "Jesus is the most persistent pedestrian in the Bible" is a quotation from IVP's excellent *Dictionary of Biblical Imagery*, page 922. I've drawn heavily in this letter from the two articles on "Walk, Walking" and "Path."

The Pilgrim's Progress is available in many editions, both print and electronic. My quotations are all from the Banner of Truth edition listed in the bibliography.

Letter 2: Turning to God. Luther's affirmation that all of life is repentance is from The Ninety-Five Theses in *Martin Luther: Selections from His Writings*, page 490.

The quotation from Thomas Watson is found in *The Doctrine of Repentance*, page 22.

Letter 3: The Noonday Demon. All allusions and quotations from ancient and classical writers in this letter are found in R. R. Reno's article, "Fighting the Noonday Devil."

Dorothy Sayers's helpful essay offers a needed corrective to those who think of immorality mostly in terms of sexual sin while neglecting the other six deadly sins (namely, wrath, gluttony, covetousness, envy, sloth, and pride). This perceptive comment on how sloth masquerades as busyness is on page 176 of *The Whimsical Christian*, but the whole essay is well worth reading.

Bunyan's picture of the continually burning fire is found in *The Pilgrim's Progress*, pages 29–30.

Letter 4: Walking in the Spirit. Bunyan's image of the dusty room is from *The Pilgrim's Progress*, pages 26–27.

"Run, John, run" is often cited in books and sermons and has been attributed to both John Bunyan and John Berridge, but I have been unable to locate its original source.

"It's not in trying, but in trusting" is from Larnelle Harris's song, "The Strength of the Lord."

Lewis's quotation on prayer is from his delightful, posthumously published *Letters to Malcolm: Chiefly on Prayer*, page 69.

Owen's study on the Holy Spirit is exhaustive in scope (and thus exhausting to read!), comprising nine "books" and filling two full volumes in his *Works*. This quotation is from volume 3, page 204.

The quotation from Edwards is found in his notebook on "Efficacious Grace," published in *Writings on the Trinity, Grace, and Faith* in *The Works of Jonathan Edwards*, volume 21, page 251.

Letter 5: Counterfeit Faith. Yes, more Bunyan! The "Way to Hell from the Gates of Heaven" statement is found on page 189 of *The Pilgrim's Progress*, while the Giant Despair episode is from pages 128–135.

Letter 6: Hope in God. Aquinas discusses thoroughly the relationship between sloth and sorrow in *Summa Theologica*, II-II. Q. 35, but for a brief historical overview of sloth, see chapter 8 in Solomon Schimmel's *The Seven Deadly Sins* (a helpful overview of the seven deadly sins in classical, Jewish, and Christian thought from a psychologist's perspective). The best contemporary study on the seven deadly sins from a Christian perspective is Rebecca Konyndyk DeYoung's *Glittering Vices: A New Look at the Seven Deadly Sins and Their Remedies*.

Mchugh, Phill, "The Strength Of The Lord," Copyright © 1987 River Oaks Music Company (BMI) (adm. at CapitolCMGPublishing.com) All rights reserved. Used by permission. Song ID:8257. International Copyright Secured. All Rights Reserved. Used by Permission.

Letter 7: The Danger of Apostasy. Lewis's counsel on reading old books is found in two places: his introduction to Athanasius's *On the Incarnation* and his essay "On the Reading of Old Books" collected in *God in the Dock*.

I'll refer to Schreiner and Caneday's book several times in these letters. It remains the best exegetical, biblical, and theological work on the doctrines of perseverance and assurance that I've read.

Letter 8: The Price of Neglect. John Cassian was the fourth– and fifth-century Roman monk and contemporary of Augustine who (following Evagrius of Pontus) catalogued the eight capital sins. Gregory the Great later condensed the list to seven in his *Morals on the Book of Job*. My quotations from Cassian are found in his *Institutes*, X.1, 3.

Screwtape's diabolical advice to Wormwood is from the twelfth letter in Lewis's *The Screwtape Letters*.

Dorothy Sayers's description of acedia is on page 176 of *The Whimsical Christian*.

The delightful scene from Juster's *The Phantom Tollbooth* is on pages 22–31.

Letter 9: Is Salvation Unconditional? Schreiner and Caneday discuss the multi-faceted metaphors for salvation on pages 46–86 of *The Race Set Before Us* and the nature of conditions on pages 40–43.

The actual quotations from Augustine's *Confessions* are "Give what you command, and then command what you will" (X.29, page 263) and "Strengthen me too, that I may be capable, give what you command, and then command whatever you will. . . . These texts make it clear, O holy God, my God, that when what you command is done, it is by your gift" (X.31, page 267).

Toplady's hymn "A Debtor to Mercy Alone" was written in 1771.

Piper's helpful unpacking of "Unmerited, Conditional, Future Grace" is in Part VI of *Future Grace*.

Letter 10: The Danger of Backsliding. In *Greek Grammar Beyond the Basics,* Daniel Wallace says that a first class condition "indicates the assumption of truth for the sake of argument" (page 450).

Octavius Winslow's *Personal Declension and Revival of Religion in the Soul* is both deeply convicting and hope giving. In it, Winslow examines declension in love, faith, prayer, and doctrine with the diagnostic proficiency of a true physician of souls, and he skillfully prescribes remedies for personal revival. This quotation is from page 100.

Don King, in a thoughtful essay on "Narnia and the Seven Deadly Sins," suggested that Lewis specifically targeted the sin of sloth in *The Silver Chair*. My Quotations from *The Silver Chair* are from pages 21 and 157.

Letter 11: Profile of an Apostate. Thomas Brooks is one of the most engaging and easy-to-read Puritan authors. This quotation from *Heaven on Earth,* a pastoral treatise on assurance, is found in *The Works of Thomas Brooks,* volume 2, page 387.

The quotation from Bradley is on page 13 in his *Shakespearean Tragedy*.

For Bunyan's chilling episode concerning the man in the iron cage, see *The Pilgrim's Progress*, pages 31–32.

Lewis's description of the damned is found in chapter 13 of *The Great Divorce*.

The John Owen quotation is found on pages 567–568 in volume 6 of his *Works*.

Letter 12: The Divine Lover. "O to grace how great a debtor" is verse 4 of Robert Robinson's 1758 hymn "Come, Thou Fount of Every Blessing."

The quotations from Jeremiah 3 are from the NIV.

Ray Ortlund's *God's Unfaithful Wife: A Biblical Theology of Spiritual Adultery* is biblical theology at its pastoral best. This quotation is from page 173.

"Then beneath the cross adoring" comes from an obscure hymn, "On the Wings of Faith Uprising," which J. Swain wrote in 1858. I came across it in Octavius Winslow's *Personal Declension*.

Letter 13: Intervening Grace. Steve Turner chronicled the life of Johnny Cash in his biography, *A Man Called Cash*. The quotation is from page 173.

You can watch the video for "Hurt" at: http://www.youtube.com/watch?v=SmVAWKfJ4Go (Accessed February 17, 2014).

The quotations from Jeremiah in this letter are from the NIV.

C. S. Lewis wrote that sentence in *The Problem of Pain*, page 33.

On how Ambrose helped Augustine, see *Confessions,* Book V, Chapter 20.

Owen's counsel for seeking an able spiritual guide is in his *Works*, page 239 of volume 7.

Letter 14: A Lifting Up for the Downcast. William Bridge's classic treatment of spiritual depression is one of the few books to which I frequently return. These quotations are from pages 69–71, 81–83, and 170–171.

Letter 15: The Wounded Surgeon. The quotation from Pascal is number 657 in his *Pensées* (page 323 of the edition cited in the bibliography).

These stanzas are from the fourth section of "East Coker" in T. S. Eliot's *Four Quartets*.

Luther's thoughts on the journey are from his "Argument in Defense of All the Articles of Dr. Martin Luther Wrongly Condemned in the Roman Bull," published in 1521.

Letter 16: The Good Fight of Faith. Annie Dillard wrote the story about John Franklin's expedition on pages 24–26 of her *Teaching a Stone to Talk: Expeditions and Encounters*.

Warren Wiersbe described the Christian life as a battlefield rather than a playground in his commentary on Philippians (page 633 of the edition cited in the bibliography).

J. C. Ryle was a nineteenth-century evangelical Anglican bishop whose classic book on holiness was, in part, a polemic against the burgeoning Higher Life movement. Ryle was concerned with this movement's overly passive approach to sanctification. For his rousing exposition of the Christian's fight, see chapter 4 in *Holiness: Its Nature, Hindrances, Difficulties, and Roots*. This quotation is from pages 53–54.

All of the Luther quotations, of course, are from "Ein feste Burg ist unser Got," translated to English by Frederick H. Hedge in 1853 as "A Mighty Fortress is Our God."

Letter 17: Put on the Gospel Armor. For details on the commentaries, see the bibliography. The quotation about *panoplia* is from page 442 of Lincoln's commentary on Ephesians.

Gurnall's gigantic exposition of the Christian armor is really a Puritan body of practical divinity, a manual for Christian living. The quotation is from volume 1, pages 63–64.

"Put on the gospel armor" is a line from the fourth verse of George Duffield Jr.'s 1858 hymn "Stand Up, Stand Up for Jesus."

Letter 18: Rightly Ordered Loves. Calvin calls our hearts idol factories in the *Institutes* I.XI.8 (page 108).

Lewis's essay "First and Second Things" is found in *God in the Dock*. This quotation is from page 280.

In this letter (excerpted from page 391 in volume II of Lewis's *Collected Letters*), Lewis applies what Denis De Rougemont wrote about art to sensual love: "It ceases to be a devil when it ceases to be a god."

Carson calls sin the "de-godding of God" in *Christ and Culture Revisited,* page 46.

The quotations from Augustine are from *De Doctrina Christiana,* or *Teaching Christianity,* Book I (page 118 in my edition cited in the bibliography), and *The City of God,* Book 15, chapter 22. See also chapter 5 on "The Order of Love" in John Burnaby's classic study of Augustine, *Amor Dei: A Study of the Religion of St. Augustine* and chapter 27 in Peter Brown's *Augustine of Hippo: A Biography.* For a book-length treatment of rightly-ordered loves, see David K. Naugle, *Reordered Love, Reordered Lives: Learning the Deep Meaning of Happiness.*

Lots of C. S. Lewis in this letter! The excerpt about Aslan and Bacchus is from *Prince Caspian,* chapter 11. The quotation from *The Great Divorce* is from chapter 11, while the postscript from *The Screwtape Letters* is from Letter 9. I'm grateful for Corbin Scott Carnell for making some of these connections in a chapter called "The Location of Joy" within his *Bright Shadow of Reality: Spiritual Longing in C. S. Lewis.*

Letter 19. Enjoying God in Everything. The quotation from Augustine is from *City of God,* Book XXII, chapter 24, as quoted on page 329 of Brown's *Augustine of Hippo: A Biography.*

Lewis's reflections on pleasure come from pages 89–91 in *Letters to Malcolm: Chiefly on Prayer.*

I've quoted only the first and last of six stanzas in Herbert's "The Elixir," found on page 174 in his *Complete Poems.*

The closing Edwards quotation is from his sermon "The Christian Pilgrim," found in volume 2, page 244, of the Dwight edition of his *Works.*

Letter 20: Spiritual Blahs. This quotation comes from page 178 in Lamott's *Bird by Bird.*

Letter 21: The Proper End and Design of Evangelical Truths. O'Connor referred to her first novel this way in a letter published on page 891 of her *Collected Works.*

Owen's discussion on the proper end of evangelical truth is on pages 82–85 in volume 7 of his *Works*.

Dillard's musings on weasels is from *Teaching a Stone to Talk*, pages 11–12 and 70.

Letter 22: Embracing Community. The Bonhoeffer quotations are from pages 26–27 of *Life Together*.

Letter 23: Assurance of Salvation. I have borrowed and adapted the stool image from page 276 of Schreiner and Caneday's *The Race Set Before Us*. "Our assurance in faith," write the authors, "depends on a three-legged stool: (1) God's promises (2) the fruit of the Spirit in our lives and (3) the witness of the Holy Spirit." I have suggested a fourth leg to the stool: the fruit of love in relationships with other believers. But such love is obviously included in the fruit of the Spirit as well.

Owen's exhortation about not mixing foundation work with building work is from pages 564–566 in volume 6 of his *Works*.

Letter 24: The Subtle Danger of Self-Trust. Spurgeon talks about the Arbor of Sloth in his sermon "Enchanted Ground," published in *The New Park Street Pulpit*, volume 2, pages 81-88.

I've quoted the first three of four verses from Edwards Mote's 1834 hymn "My Hope is Built."

The Owen quotation is from pages 460–461 in volume 1 of his *Works*.

Letter 25: Developing a Spiritual Growth Plan. Consider for example the Bible reading plan devised by 19th century Scottish minister, Robert Murray M'Cheyne, which takes you through the Old Testament once and the New Testament and Psalms twice, reading roughly four chapters a day. The plan is available online at: http://www.esv.org/assets/pdfs/rp.one.year.tract.pdf. Accessed March 31, 2014.

Letter 26: Gospel Humility. The Bunyan quotation is from page 182 in *Grace Abounding to the Chief of Sinners*.

For Ryle's arguments against the "let go and let God" theology of the Keswick movement, see especially his introduction to *Holiness*.

Letter 27: Resting in Jesus. The famous quotation from Augustine is from *Confessions*, Book I, Chapter 1.

"Cast your deadly 'doing' down" is from James Proctor's nineteenth-century hymn "It is Finished."

The monkey and jar illustration from John Piper is on page 313 in the first edition of *Future Grace*.

Letter 28: The Race Set Before Us. John Piper quoted Spurgeon's remark on orthodoxy and piety in his biographical lecture "Charles Spurgeon: Preaching through Adversity."

Lewis's comment about the devotional value of reading theology is part of his essay "On the Reading of Old Books" collected in *God in the Dock*, page 205.

Bunyan's *The Heavenly Footman* is much less famous than *The Pilgrim's Progress,* but it is a short, convicting, and challenging book. My quotations are from pages 31, 33, and 30, respectively.

The hymn verses are from Isaac Watts's early eighteenth-century hymn "Awake, Our Souls, Away, Our Fears."

See Fee's commentary (listed in bibliography) pages 465–470 and 534–569.

Letter 29: Looking to Jesus. John Calvin wrote much about the Lord's Table. My quotations are from his *Short Treatise on the Holy Supper of Our Lord and Only Savior Jesus Christ* in *Theological Treatises*. See especially pages 152–153.

William Barclay's translation of 1 Cornthians 9:27 is on page 85 of his commentary on *The Letters to the Corinthians*.

Letter 30: *Vincit Qui Patitur.* J. I. Packer's discussion of *Vincit Qui Patitur* is found on page 22 of *Faithfulness and Holiness: The Witness of J. C. Ryle*. This book also contains the text of Ryle's first edition of *Holiness*, and the quotation about overcoming is from page 54 of *Holiness*.

Christian's exchange with the Porter of the Lodge is on page 45 of *The Pilgrim's Progress*, and his discussion with Prudence is on page 51.

Letter 31: The Preservation of the Saints. "Before the Throne of God Above" was written by Charitie L. Bancroft in 1863.

Bibliography

Aquinas, Thomas. *Summa Theologica*. Vols. 19–20, *Great Books of the Western World*, edited by Robert Maynard Hutchins. Chicago: Encyclopedia Britannica, 1952.

Augustine. *City of God*. Translated by Henry Bettenson. New York: Penguin Books, 2003.

___. *The Confessions*. Translated by Maria Boulding. New York: New City, 1997.

—. *Teaching Christianity (On Christian Doctrine)*. Translated by Edmund Hill. New York: New City, 1996.

The Baptist Confession of 1689. http://spurgeon.org/~phil/creeds/bcof.htm. Accessed January 17, 2013.

Barclay, William. *The Letters to the Corinthians*, rev. ed. Philadelphia: Westminster, 1975.

The Belgic Confession. http://www.crcna.org/welcome/beliefs/confessions/belgic-confession. Accessed January 17, 2013.

Bonhoeffer, Dietrich. *The Cost of Discipleship*. New York: Harper, 1954.

—. *Life Together: The Classic Exploration of Faith in Community*. San Francisco: HarperSanFrancisco, 1954.

Bradley, A. C. *Shakespearean Tragedy: Lectures on Hamlet, Othello, King Lear, and Macbeth*. New York: Barnes & Noble, 2005.

Bridge, William. *A Lifting Up for the Downcast*. Carlisle, PA: Banner of Truth, 1961.

Brooks, Thomas. *Heaven on Earth*. Vol 2, *The Works of Thomas Brooks*, edited by Alexander B. Grossart. Carlisle: PA: Banner of Truth, 1980.

Brown, Peter. *Augustine of Hippo: A Biography*. Berkeley: University of California, 2000.

Bunyan, John. *Grace Abounding to the Chief of Sinners*. Westwood, NJ: Barbour, 1998.

—. *The Heavenly Footman: A Puritan's View of How to Get to Heaven*. Ross-shire, Great Britain: Christian Focus, 2002.

—. *The Pilgrim's Progress*. Carlisle, PA: Banner of Truth, 1977.

Burnaby, John. *Amor Dei: A Study of the Religion of St. Augustine*. Eugene, OR: Wipf & Stock, 2007.

Calvin, John. *Institutes of the Christian Religion*. Edited by John T. McNeil. Translated by Ford L. Battles. Philadelphia: Westminster, 1960.

—. *Short Treatise on the Holy Supper of Our Lord and Only Savior Jesus Christ*. In *Calvin: Theological Treatises*, edited by J. K. S. Reid. Philadelphia: Westminster, 1954.

Carson, D. A. *Christ and Culture Revisited*. Grand Rapids, MI: Eerdmans, 2008.

Cassian, John. *The Institutes of John Cassian*. Translated by Edgar C. S. Gibson. In Vol. 11 of *Nicene and Post-Nicene Fathers*, Series 2, 4th ed., edited by Philip Schaff. Peabody, MA: Hendrickson, 2004.

Chambers, Oswald. *My Utmost for His Highest*. Grand Rapids, MI: Discovery House, 1992.

Carnell, Corbin Scott. *Bright Shadow of Reality: Spiritual Longing in C. S. Lewis*. Grand Rapids, MI: Eerdmans, 1999.

DeYoung, Rebecca Konyndyk. *Glittering Vices: A New Look at the Seven Deadly Sins and Their Remedies*. Grand Rapids, MI: Brazos Press, 2009.

Dillard, Annie. *Teaching a Stone to Talk: Expeditions and Encounters*. New York: Harper, 1982.

Dillenberger, John ed., *Martin Luther: Selections from His Writings*. New York: Anchor, 1962.

Edwards, Jonathan. "The Christian Pilgrim." In Vol. 2, *The Works of Jonathan Edwards*, edited by Sereno Dwight. Carlisle, PA: Banner of Truth, 1974.

—. *Letters and Personal Writings*. Vol. 16, *The Works of Jonathan Edwards*, edited by George S. Claghorn. New Haven, CT: Yale University Press, 1998.

—. *Writings on the Trinity, Grace, and Faith*. Vol. 21, *The Works of Jonathan Edwards*, edited by Sang Hyan Lee. New Haven, CT: Yale University Press, 2003.

Eliot, T. S. *Four Quartets*. Orlando, FL: Mariner, 1968.

Fee, Gordon D. *The First Epistle to the Corinthians* (NICNT). Grand Rapids, MI: Eerdmans, 1987.

Gurnall, William. *The Christian in Complete Armor*. Carlisle, PA: Banner of Truth, 1964.

Hedges, Brian G. *Christ Formed in You: The Power of the Gospel for Personal Change*. Wapwallopen, PA: Shepherd Press, 2010.

Herbert, George. *The Complete English Poems*. New York: Penguin, 2004.

Horton, Michael. *Putting Amazing Back into Grace*. Grand Rapids, MI: Baker, 1994.

Juster, Norton. *The Phantom Tollbooth*. New York: Random House, 1972.

Keller, Timothy. "All of Life Is Repentance." http://download.redeemer. com/pdf/learn/resources/All_of_Life_Is_Repentance-Keller.pdf. Accessed February 17, 2014.

King, Don W. "Narnia and the Seven Deadly Sins." *Mythlore* 10 (Spring 1984): 14–19. Reprinted at http://cslewis.drzeus.net/papers/7sins.html. Accessed February 17, 2014.

Lamott, Anne. *Bird by Bird: Some Instructions on Writing and Life*. New York: Anchor, 1995.

Lewis, C. S. *The Collected Letters of C. S. Lewis*. Edited by Walter Hooper. Volume II: *Books, Broadcasts, and the War, 1931–1949*. New York: HarperCollins, 2004.

—. *The Great Divorce: A Dream*. New York: HarperCollins, 1973.

—. *God in the Dock: Essays in Theology and Ethics*. Grand Rapids, MI: Eerdmans, 1970.

—. Introduction to *On the Incarnation*, by Athanasius. Crestwood, NY: St. Vladimir's Seminary Press, 1977.

—. *Letters to Malcolm: Chiefly on Prayer*. New York: Harcourt, 1991.

—. *The Pilgrim's Regress: An Allegorical Apology for Christianity, Reason, and Romanticism*. Grand Rapids, MI: Eerdmans, 1958.

—. *Prince Caspian*. New York: Collier, 1970.

—. *The Problem of Pain*. New York: HarperCollins, 1996.

—. *The Silver Chair*. New York: Collier, 1970.

—. *The Screwtape Letters*. New York: HarperCollins, 2001.

—. *Surprised by Joy: The Shape of My Early Life*. New York: Harcourt, 1984.

Lincoln, Andrew T. *Word Biblical Commentary: Ephesians*. Dallas, TX: Word, 1990.

Lloyd-Jones, D. Martyn. *Spiritual Depression: Its Causes and Cure*. Grand Rapids, MI: Eerdmans, 1965.

Luther, Martin. "An Argument in Defense of All the Articles of Dr. Martin Luther Wrongly Condemned in the Roman Bull," in *Works of Martin Luther*, vol. 3. Albany, OR: AGES Software, 1997.

—. *Letters of Spiritual Counsel*. Vol. 18, *The Library of Christian Classics*, edited by Theodore G. Tappert. Louisville, KY: Westminster, 1955.

—. "The Ninety-Five Theses." *Martin Luther: Selections from His Writings*, edited by John Dillenberger. New York: Anchor, 1962.

Naugle, David K. *Reordered Love, Reordered Lives: Learning the Deep Meaning of Happiness*. Grand Rapids, MI: Eerdmans, 2008.

Newton, John. *Cardiphonia: Or, The Utterance of the Heart: In a Real Correspondence*. Vols. 1 and 2, *The Works of John Newton*. Carlisle, PA: Banner of Truth, 1988.

O'Connor, Flannery. *Collected Works*. New York: Library of America, 1988.

Ortlund, Raymond C. *God's Unfaithful Wife: A Biblical Theology of Spiritual Adultery*. Downers Grove, IL: InterVarsity, 1996.

Owen, John. *A Discourse Concerning the Holy Spirit*. Vol. 3, *The Works of John Owen*, edited by William H. Gould. Carlisle, PA: Banner of Truth, 1967.

—. *The Doctrine of the Saints' Perseverance Explained and Confirmed*. Vol. 11, *The Works of John Owen*, edited by William H. Gould. Carlisle, PA: Banner of Truth, 1967.

—. *Meditations and Discourses Concerning the Glory of Christ; Applied unto Unconverted Sinners and Saints under Spiritual Decays*. Vol. 1, *The Works of John Owen*, edited by William H. Gould. Carlisle, PA: Banner of Truth, 1967.

—. *Nature and Causes of Apostasy from the Gospel*. Vol. 7, *The Works of John Owen*, edited by William H. Gould. Carlisle, PA: Banner of Truth, 1967.

—. *A Practical Exposition Upon Psalm CXXX*. Vol. 6, *The Works of John Owen*, edited by William H. Gould. Carlisle, PA: Banner of Truth, 1967.

Packer, J. I. *Faithfulness and Holiness: The Witness of J. C. Ryle*. Wheaton, IL: Crossway, 2002.

—. *Keep in Step with the Spirit*. Grand Rapids, MI: Fleming H. Revell, 1984.

Pascal, Blaise. *Pensées*. Translated by A. J. Krailsheimer. New York: Penguin, 1966.

Piper, John. "Charles Spurgeon: Preaching through Adversity." http://www.desiringgod.org/biographies/charles-spurgeon-preaching-through-adversity. Accessed February 20, 2013.

—. *The Purifying Power of Living by Faith in Future Grace*. Sisters, OR: Multnomah, 1995.

Reno, R. R. "Fighting the Noonday Devil." *First Things*, August/September 2003. http://www.firstthings.com/article/2007/01/fighting-the-noonday-devil. Accessed February 17, 2014. Reprinted in *Fighting the Noonday Devil—and Other Essays Personal and Theological*. Grand Rapids, MI: Eerdmans, 2011.

Ryken, Leland et al., eds. *Dictionary of Biblical Imagery*. Downers Grove, IL: InterVarsity, 2000.

Ryle, J. C. *Holiness: Its Nature, Hindrances, Difficulties, and Roots*. Darlington, England: Evangelical, 1997.

Sayers, Dorothy L. "The Other Six Deadly Sins." *The Whimsical Christian: 18 Essays*. New York: Macmillan, 1978.

Schimmel, Solomon. *The Seven Deadly Sins: Jewish, Christian, and Classical Reflections on Human Psychology*. New York: Oxford University Press, 1997.

Schreiner, Thomas R., and Ardel B. Caneday. *The Race Set Before Us: A Biblical Theology of Perseverance and Assurance*. Downers Grove, IL: InterVarsity, 2001.

Spurgeon, C. H. "Enchanted Ground." Vol. 2, *The New Park Street Pulpit*. Grand Rapids, MI: Baker, 1994.

Turner, Steve. *A Man Called Cash: The Life, Love, and Faith of an American Legend*. Nashville, TN: Thomas Nelson. 2004.

Wallace, Daniel B. *Greek Grammar Beyond the Basics: An Exegetical Syntax of the New Testament*. Grand Rapids, MI: Zondervan, 1996.

Watson, Thomas. *The Doctrine of Repentance*. Carlisle, PA: Banner of Truth, 1987.

Wiersbe, Warren. *The Wiersbe Bible Commentary: New Testament*. Colorado Springs: David C. Cook, 2007.

Winslow, Octavius. *Personal Declension and Revival of Religion in the Soul*. Carlisle, PA: Banner of Truth, 2009.

Westminster Confession of Faith. http://www.reformed.org/documents/wcf_with_proofs. Accessed January 17, 2013.

Westminster Larger Catechism. http://www.reformed.org/documents/wlc_w_proofs. Accessed January 17, 2013.

Connect with
BRIAN
Hedges

Read more at Brian's blog:
www.brianghedges.com
Sermons: www.fulkersonpark.com/audio

 @brianghedges

 www.facebook.com/brian.g.hedges